Words for Letters

Writing Personal Letters For Deeper Friendships

Keith Winnard

Words for Letters

Words for Letters:

Writing Personal Letters For Deeper Friendships

First Published 2014

Self-Published by Keith Winnard

First Edition

The author asserts the moral rights to be identified as the author of this work.

ISBN-13: 978-1497534469

ISBN-10: 1497534461

Printed by CreateSpace.

Copyright © Keith Winnard 2014

Photographs and Cover Design Copyright © Jane Peeks 2014

All rights reserved. No part of this publication may be reproduced, stored in a retrieval system, or transmitted in any form or by any means, electronic, mechanical, photocopying, recording or otherwise without the prior permission of the copyright owner.

Dedication

To anyone who has held a pen

and made souls dance.

Words for Letters

TABLE OF CONTENTS

	Acknowledgements		v
	Introduction		vi
Part 1			
1	Words, Words, and Words		1
2	Prepare Yourself		6
3	Basic Letter Layout		24
Part 2			
4	Letters are more than just Words		36
5	A Letter of Congratulations		44
6	A Letter of Invitation		52
7	A Thank You Letter		60
8	A Letter to Rekindle a Friendship		65
9	A Letter of Comfort		71
10	A Letter of Encouragement		76
11	A Letter of Condolence		81
12	A Letter of Recommendation		90
13	A Letter of Vengeance		94
14	A Letter of Apology		95
15	The Annual Holiday Letter		99
16	A Love Letter		108
17	A Letter of Curiosity		113
18	A Letter of General Correspondence		118
Part 3			
19	Replying to a Letter		121
20	Personal Letter Writing Skills		126
21	Fun with Letters		131
22	Reading Letters		136
23	The Closing		140

Acknowledgements

I acknowledge the following people for the role played either knowingly or unknowingly, in making this book possible:

Derek Liggins, longtime friend and mentor, who insisted I write this book and subsequently encouraged me all the way through to publication.

Rev. W. A. Parker, who in September 1967, taught our class how to write letters to our families and gave us advice and guidance to improve our handwriting.

Jane Peeks, for her photography skills, book cover design and creation, and the assistance of Tracey, Lorna, Binx, Derek, Kyrie, and Rosie.

Thanks to Pamela Nealey Gress for editing the manuscript and her encouragement.

Introduction

A handwritten personal letter unexpectedly appears in your mailbox. You pick up the envelope. Who sent this? Where has it come from? Why has someone written to *you*? It's not your birthday. What has happened? Is it an invitation? Have you forgotten a special date? Your fingers detect an object hidden in the envelope... something purposefully concealed. What is it?

The envelope in your hand did not fall into your mailbox by chance; someone willfully sent it to you. It's not just another mailshot, not a circular. No, this is very special. Someone has dedicated time to sharing thoughts with you in a personal way. Someone – at this point unknown – added warmth to these thoughts and wants to let you know you are special. He, she or they made this effort for *you!*

What feelings does this envelope create in you? Do you feel the same way about each email message you receive in your inbox or through social media? I suspect we both probably have the same answer to that question.

You are holding all the answers to these questions. Go ahead and open it and all will be revealed.

Clean up your Boxes

Attention please! We must start by turning your postal mailbox into a more pleasant place to visit. This is only fair; if someone is making a special and friendly effort to write to us, we should reciprocate by ensuring we can easily receive their mail. We do not want to lose it amongst the clutter of junk mail which can frequently amass and soon become out of control.

The first step is to stop the junk mail by requesting to be taken off the sender's marketing distribution lists. Secondly, reduce the amount of printed mail by redirecting it to an email account. You will be surprised at how effective these two actions are at freeing up your mailbox, creating additional room to receive more welcoming and interesting correspondence.

Handwritten Personal Letters

Imagine handwritten envelopes addressed to you appearing regularly in your mailbox. What might each contain? Perhaps you are invited to a party or maybe a friend has replied to one of your letters.

These arrivals are small bundles of joy waiting to be savored and loved; personal letters from friends delivered to you. So much joy is waiting for you. Your friends will share your emotions knowing you are reading their words. Be sure to reciprocate by replying to each letter you receive. Spread the happiness; all you have to do is to pick up your pen and start writing. As your skills and enthusiasm grow, so too will the appreciation of your friends. You will become more popular.

How are you going to achieve this?

This book takes you through easy to follow steps. You will write your first letter very soon. You may feel a little overwhelmed or uncomfortable about putting pen to paper because you simply do not know what to say, or you may see letter writing as difficult. This book will help you to develop your personal letter writing skills.

Different occasions or circumstances call for particular types of letters. Several kinds of letters are included in Part 2 to help you start off successfully. We all have to begin somewhere; this is your chance to learn and develop your letter writing skills. Not only that, you will naturally introduce other people into this delightful and highly rewarding pastime.

How to use this book.

This book is divided into three parts and aims to have you writing in no time at all. In a nutshell, it looks like this:

- ❖ Part 1
  - ➢ Setting up headquarters!
  - ➢ The basic letter and envelope layout.
  - ➢ Your handwriting.
- ❖ Part 2
  - ➢ Overcome doubts and fears; open the doors to joy.
  - ➢ See how to write various types of personal letters.
- ❖ Part 3
  - ➢ Reading and replying to letters.
  - ➢ Developing your skills and having fun!

As you progress through the book make notes in the margins, highlight whatever you like, and underline words that are important to *you*.

One goal

This book has one goal - To help you and your friends start experiencing the delights of both writing and reading personal letters.

If you are new to this, you have the right book in your hand. Your friends will see a new side to you. Personal letters add a little more quality to your life. Perhaps you are already experienced, then use this book to inspire you and develop more creative ways to enrich your ties with those you care for.

So, if you are ready to step into this enjoyable world, continue reading and let us enjoy some time together.

Good Luck!

Part 1

Chapter 1

Words, Words, and Words

The proper definition of a man is an animal that writes letters.
~ Lewis Carroll ~

There are words, then there are words, and then there are words. There is also nothing like a clear and simple start to the first chapter and this – as they say – is nothing of the sort. Stay with me and allow me to untangle the mystery behind such a puzzling proclamation.

Impact

Words do have an effect on us. They can change how we see things. What feelings does the word "Congratulations!" stir up inside of you? How about "Sorry'"? Is that the same feeling? No of course not. The two words spark two very different emotions within us.

Two other words which can not only change our mood but possibly our whole life are "thank you". A growing sense of gratitude to those around us can have a profound effect on all concerned and in many aspects of our lives.

Words for Letters

Let us suppose for a moment, that you invite friends around to your house for a dinner party to celebrate your birthday. At the end of the dinner your guests leave. You hear, *"Thanks for a great time."* and soon afterwards you receive a text or social media message relating the same words or close to that. You understand exactly what that means. The electronic messages say what they need to say and that is that, a very functional, courteous, and efficient way of expressing thanks. The more adventurous guests may expand the message to *"Thank you so much, we had a fabulous time."* Once again, simple and straight forward and it does express a little more appreciation and gratitude. Moving from the adventurous to daring you might receive a letter a day or two later.

12th January 2014

Dear Emma,

Thank you for such a lovely evening. We are all agreed that nobody has your magical touch with pasta. What a wonderful dinner; Dave and Marie must have set a record for second (and third) helpings! I hear that Alex is still singing your praises. How do you make it seem so effortless?

I have enclosed a photograph of all of us together on the night and will send a copy to the others too, so we all have a memory of your fantastic birthday party.

Thank you so much for treating us to an unforgettable meal and for such a wonderful evening shared with friends celebrating your 21st birthday for the 22nd time! You just get better and better each year.

See you soon,

Paul.

If you were Emma, which expression of gratitude touches you the most? How does the text, message and the letter make you feel? The time and effort to write each one differs but that little extra effort and the addition of a photograph makes a significant difference in the effect on Emma. In the above scenario Paul has made more of a personal effort to not just express appreciation and gratitude but also to affirm friendship by adding warmth to his words. He also brings into play the group of friends being together. No doubt, in the above scenario, Paul would have thanked Emma verbally on the night too. The letter he chose to write enriches the whole birthday experience for her.

Email, Social Media, and Messaging

Why would you consider writing a letter instead of communicating electronically? Good question. After all, electronic communication is easier and quicker. In addition, you already have all the materials you need at your fingertips. Emails, texts, social networks are unbeatable for circulating information quickly and simultaneously. You can reach out instantly to friends or a group of people with related interests and receive prompt responses. New technologies are ideal for gauging interest quickly, making arrangements, easily tracking where people are, and much more. The *here and now* age of information hastens our lives. So much data, facts, opinions, news, and thoughts stream non-stop to and from our devices, efficiency and convenience all rolled into one. We live in a truly remarkable and ever-advancing technological age.

Life is not all about efficiency and convenience though, is it? The increasing pace of living does not necessarily enrich our lives; in some instances individuals find it tiring, overwhelming and stressful. Change of pace has to be the key to a more fulfilled life. We are humans; we all have a choice.

Let us compare the instant technology delivery with personal letter writing. You may eat regularly in fast food outlets, but what about the special occasions? Suppose you want to spend a special evening out with your friend. Would you prefer a fast food outlet or a visit to a restaurant? The restaurant experience is akin to writing a letter. You prefer to take your time, relax, relish the food, and enjoy the evening spending quality time together. You want to prepare for what you are going to say, chew over a few ideas, serve up your thoughts onto the paper, and produce a tasteful communication – not literally of course; they may find your words hard to digest – which will thrill your reader. Writing a letter is an act of friendship; a way of harmonizing with those you care about.

Should you replace all your electronic communication with handwritten letters? No, that would not be practical or maybe even possible. Is there a clear line when one method is preferable over the other? Not really. Once you start writing letters your feelings and the circumstances will let you know which option to take. You can choose to write a letter on your word processor and attach it to an email. This is fine if hand writing the letter is not possible. Sometimes we have to make a decision that we would prefer not to but given limited resources, if it is the best option at the time, so be it.

In all written communication your words portray both your message and your feelings. You are only limited by your imagination when writing with a pen. You have much more opportunity to bring the paper to life with the words you choose and the way in which you physically present them.

Letter or Note?

Are they the same? Possibly, but if you put me on the spot and demand a definite answer, I will unconditionally commit to a definite maybe that no they are not. *Why?* Yes of course they have many similarities but a note tends to lean towards a short communication and typically focuses on a single point. Letters have the capacity to undertake a wider role. In Part 2 you will see how notes and letters relating to the same circumstances can be very effective but in different ways. Having said that; some letters perfectly fit the description of a note I just gave you.

So, at the end of this chapter, it only remains for me to dodge this question and in the spirit of political rhetoric, to try to put the onus back on you! Once you reach the end of this book and have a few letters and notes under your belt, you will be better positioned to have your own definition. And that is good enough for me, because this book encourages you to reach your own decisions and to write your letters in your own unique way – that is why they will be so special.

Chapter 2

Prepare Yourself!

Let us move on, and step out boldly, though it be into the night, and we can scarcely see the way.
~ Charles B. Newcomb ~

What do you need to start? Not a lot really. Here comes the big question: *What do need more than anything else to start?* Put this book down for a minute and consider this. What are the first few thoughts? No peeping ahead  now. Jot your answer on a piece of paper. Stop reading; your minute starts now.

What do you need the most?

What are your suggestions for this? Why did you choose them? The answer below is written backwards to try to conceal it from any wandering eyes that may have stolen a glance and given away the game. My suggestion is 'ot etirw ot enoemos'. Did you arrive at the same conclusion or were you thinking about pen, paper, envelopes, stamps, and other related equipment? Well, all those things are very useful but not absolutely necessary. After all you can write a letter in the sand on a beach using a stick. One problem with this approach and possibly why it has not been too popular is that you cannot send your 'letter'. Rather you have to bring your recipient to the beach to read it. A further risk is the tide; it may partially wash away your words and your reader is left trying to piece together and make sense of what you may have said.

The Romans used a pointed instrument called a stylus to write on a wax tablet. Yes tablets existed then! They wrote their letter and instructed a messenger to deliver it directly to the addressee. Modern electronic tablets simply do not carry the same degree of authenticity and have to be frequently powered up. Neither do they fit well with the toga and garland image. It's a matter of taste; I suppose it depends which forums you prefer to visit.

You need someone to write to; plain and simple. Yes, before we start you will need to single out a victim i.e. a willing friend to whom you wish to write. This sounds simpler than it really is. Many people may spring to mind, but how do you select the friend or relative to receive your first letter?

Begin by jotting down a list of people you think worthy of your efforts. Now think about each person, your relationship with them, and their present circumstances. Has anyone had fortune smile on them recently or perhaps achieved a special goal? On the flip side maybe a friend has had a poor run of luck lately and could be feeling a bit down. Still no luck? Well is there anybody on your list you have not seen for a while and would like to be in touch with again? Writing to any of the people above would be a wonderful surprise. As you will see in Part 2, there are all sorts of letters you can write; it could be a special occasion for them or just a letter to say hello again with an invitation to meet up, share old times, and rekindle your friendship.

You do not have to choose anyone just yet. If you still are unsure, carry on reading and someone will spring to mind. Besides, you always have the option of putting all those names into a hat and drawing one out. This lucky person will have won the privilege of receiving your focus of attention and subsequent letter.

Other items are necessary before you can begin. So, let us take a look at what you need.

Words for Letters

Basic Materials

Below is the basic inventory of items you require to start your letter writing. Luckily, you will probably already have many of them; others you may need to buy but they should be inexpensive.

- Pens.
- Inks and cartridges (if you are using a fountain pen.)
- Writing paper.
- Envelopes.
- Stamps.
- Notebook and pencil.
- Scrap paper.
- Blotting paper.
- Ruler.
- Shoebox!

The addition of the shoebox to the list is an ideal starter for keeping all your materials together and to keep the letters you receive. This is your compact writing office; easily transportable too.

Assembling this collection for almost zero cost is realistic. You can avoid significant financial outlay! Yes, this is true. You may even continue to maintain a zero cost if you approach this in the right manner. How can such an enjoyable hobby be free? That secret will be revealed shortly. Let us consider each item in a little more detail.

Pens

Your have to make your first decision; are you going to use a fountain pen or a ball point? If you do not currently own a fountain pen I recommend you research them before enthusiastically dashing out to buy one. The internet is a good place to start. In addition, if you are fortuitous to have a local pen shop, pay it a visit and ask the sales assistant to show you a selection. Try each one out. The price varies considerably but reasonable quality fountain pens are out there for the price of two fast food meals. They are more than adequate for writing your letter. Your fountain pen will add grace and a touch of class to the page, flowing majestically along the lines, elegantly releasing your words onto your paper. It will look great; and you will look great too.

Beware of cheap ballpoints. They get the job done but not with the same panache as a fountain pen. You can scribble your words onto the paper with the ballpoint and say what you need to say. Even include a few doodles. All of which are perfectly acceptable.

Would you like to share a secret concerning ballpoints? Come closer. Closer still. This is strictly between the two of us; nobody else needs to know. What I am about to reveal to you may have already crossed your mind when unexplainable and mysterious moments occur. Perhaps at first you just accept the odd happening but as the frequency increases, so your suspicions grow. You notice patterns starting to emerge. You dismiss from your mind what cannot be possibly true. But it is. Your ballpoints are alive! I think you already knew this deep down but let us bring it out into the open. Yes, each and every one of them has a life of its own. Where is the evidence? Leave a ball point on a table at home, on a desk at work, in fact just about anywhere, and walk away for a minute or two. On your return – you know what is coming next don't you? – yes, on your return, it has gone, vanished into thin air. Broken free and fled. You are left pen-less in your moment of need. Deserted by an impudent implement, you feel abandoned and frustrated. Who could blame you for feeling upset and deflated? You brought this ballpoint into your life, cared for it, gave it the write life. You and your ballpoint were happy together, (or so you thought) until now. Quite simply your ballpoint has forsaken you without even leaving you a letter of explanation.

Please do not judge your ex-ballpoint too harshly. They disappear for reasons. You may have bitten or chewed on it from time to time. Whether intentional or not, this is an act of aggression, one that ballpoints find difficult to defend themselves against or to counter-attack. It is an indisputable fact that ballpoints do suffer from a high kidnap rate. Research suggests ballpoints are prone to Stockholm syndrome; they soon form a new bond with their kidnappers. However, if your escapee left of its own accord then do look immediately into the surrounding nooks and crannies. Over fifty years, of personal experience with sudden desertions and disappearances, have demonstrated the first few minutes are the most important. Search and rescue agencies from all over the globe define this brief duration as *the crucial period*. You must act instantly. Modern professional psychological profilers advise us that absconding ballpoints are likely to head to places where there is little light. Generally they are attracted to the gaps in the sofa, under chairs, and behind cupboards. A few, and let us be thankful it is only a few, will even make perilous leaps over ten times their own size down the back of a refrigerator to make their escape. Assuming they survive the fall, they discover a cache of long lost coins and other booty. They become both hermit and miser; living static and content lives surrounded by their new found treasures.

The Nobility

Fountain pens differ from ballpoints and over time have acquired dual qualities. They have both the unwavering loyalty of a big floppy eared dog and the poise and grace of a Persian cat. Admirable traits with a settling effect on you, thus calming your urges to bite or chew them. Be warned, they can be equipped with an array of nibs which, in the event of an act of aggression could be used in retaliation as a weapon using snakelike ability to pump ink into you. So beware! Treat your fountain pen with love and respect. No need for you to worry about desperate leaps from a refrigerator. No, this noble breed of writing instruments has a likeable arrogance, proud of its ability to make readers gasp at beautifully crafted words and imaginative swirls. Your knightly pen served well by its loyal page will lead you to many adventures.

Fountain pens, can generally use a variety of nibs. When you purchase your pen, it will come with a single nib, but you can purchase more if you so wish. Quality pen emporiums (sadly these are becoming harder to find) endeavor to employ people who know what they are talking about. Their help can be invaluable. Talk to these wonderful people, their knowledge is boundless. They are always polite, very helpful, will explain what you need to know and answer any question you can ask. *Top Tip*: if the conversation veers towards component identification numbers you are out of your depth and are about to drown in technical overload. You should smile, make your purchase, and leave. Joking apart, do ask to try an assortment of pens and nibs to see which you prefer and listen carefully to the clerk's advice. It is not difficult to change the nibs; simply follow the instructions. Demonstrations on online video can help show you how to do it without frustrating yourself or angering your pen.

The nibs come with all sorts of options: fine, medium, and broad are the most common. A wider selection exists for more specialized uses, especially if you choose to venture out from chirography to dabble in calligraphy. To start, you may be better using either a fine or medium nib. Add an attractive and charming variation to your penmanship by using an italic nib; I prefer these. You do not have to be an expert in calligraphy to do this. Just practice a few letters and you will soon see the difference. Once again, ample examples and guides are available both online and in print to help you become reasonably skilled. Your handwriting will carry more appeal and add charisma to your letters.

Before we close the subject on nibs there is information of vital importance which you ought to declare to the sales clerk. Are you left-handed or right-handed? Some nibs, depending on what they are designed to achieve, need a different version to cater for left-handed people because of the angle at which the pen is held. Remember this, especially if you are buying a nib or pen as a present for a friend. Find out in advance if he or she is right or left-handed. Also consider that the shop may have to order the nib so be sure to allow for a little extra time to ensure your gift will be on time. The right handed versions are usually sold by default but it is always worthwhile checking by asking the sales clerk or emailing the online vendor.

Inks

Like you and I, your fountain pen needs to stay hydrated. Your first decision is whether to use a cartridge or converter. The converter allows you to refill your pen by drawing ink from a bottle; all very straightforward and simple. The tube-like cartridge contains ink and smoothly fits into your pen and can be removed and replaced with another cartridge when your pen runs out of ink. There are different types of cartridges so check for compatibility with your pen.

A whole technology and history is available for you to gain an understanding of how these magnificent writing tools have been developed. Investigative work will take you to the far corners of the nerd realm and has been known to give way to an obsession in the quest for enlightenment. All very interesting, but as your studies progress, try to draw the line at becoming an aficionado on the component identification numbers as mentioned earlier. Take note; this insatiable desire for more details leads you along a path of exploration you should only pursue if you wish to be excluded from social events and general conversation. For some inexplicable reason, this fascinating subject and huge warehouse of specialist data and precise information does not feature in the top ten list of hot topics for discussion at most social gatherings. So for now, keep it simple and let your expertise progress steadily. Be patient; I promise that one day you will amass extensive knowledge and have the chance to meet others like you at weekend conventions.

Do you want to use the cartridges or the converter? The ink bottle is the more traditional approach but many *'nouveau plumists'* use the cartridges. You may find that initially you can only buy the pen with the cartridge option but normally you can purchase a converter later to fit the pen. The pens generally will accept either. If you intend to keep your fountain pen with you day to day, it is easier to carry a packet of cartridges rather than transport bottles of ink, and generally less risky. What do I use? I use both. Over time I have managed to acquire several pens and mix and match them to suit the circumstances.

Words for Letters

As with pens and nibs, different types of inks are available. For now choose the straightforward fountain pen ink. Black or blue are the most common, you can also purchase many different colors. Inks can be a complicated subject too but for now stick with the regular. Cartridges also come in a variety of colors but do check to see if they are compatible with your pen. The choice between converter and cartridge is entirely yours. As your collection grows I suggest you try both.

Top Tip: if you intend to fly then be aware that if your pen is full of ink you may have a leak as the ink is pushed out through the nib due to the altitude and change in pressure. This may stain whatever clothing the pen is held in. To avoid this, let some ink out of the pen back into the bottle prior to flying, the converter gives you this advantage. Usually your pen will not be full so this is unlikely to be a problem, but it is always better to be safe than sorry.

Writing Paper

You can use just about any paper to write a letter. Writing pads are available online and from stationers office supply stores. One other option is to buy loose sheets of paper. A variety of stationery sizes are available. When starting out, you may feel a little overwhelmed by using a large paper size so choose a smaller option. Less can be more, as they say. Pick the one you feel most comfortable with. Several specialist stationery suppliers will cut the paper in half for you and it will still fit in a smaller envelope size.

Colored paper is available and may or may not have envelopes to match. Colored paper with contrasting ink enhances your letter and sets a tone appropriate to your letter's content. Use a specialist stationer; they have several paper colors available with matching envelopes. Like the pen emporiums they too employ gurus with breath-taking expertise and formidable practical know-how. They will be very helpful to you. Again, know your own depth; if your guru utters Delphi-oracle-riddle-like answers, just buy what you had in your hands before the conversation went ethereal. Take your pen with you to the stationers and see if the clerk will provide you with a few samples to experiment on. Try different colors of paper to gauge the effect, if you do have different ink colors then go ahead and have fun exploring more combinations.

Paper also comes in a diversity of materials and thicknesses. Make sure they are suitable for your pen. Ask if you can write on a few samples if you are unsure. Be mindful that a number of papers have a wax-like coating on them similar to certain greeting cards. Your pen may not produce the expected flow of ink and appear as if it is sitting on top of the paper. Avoid this where possible because it will smudge. Check also that your nib does not 'drag' or seem to snag on the paper. Always seek advice from the vendor. Ballpoints do not generally have the same problems and will normally write on most surfaces; they are a useful backup to your fountain pen.

Envelopes

The guardians who shield your words play a magnificent role. We underestimate their contribution to life. Torn open and discarded on arrival, and then thrown into the nearest basket. Not much of a reward for safeguarding a personal message perhaps from across the globe right into your hand. How sad for these poor uncomplaining word carriers. Envelopes perform a similar role to people who have maintenance jobs: rarely seen, seldom heard, without proper recognition but essential to any operation. Infamy is theirs when services flounder from time to time. Delivered to the wrong address, incorrect information, insufficient postage degrades the reputations of these fine upstanding workhorses. Be considerate when writing, sealing, or opening an envelope, they are there to help you. Be sure to give your envelop the right information and to diligently equip it for the journey ahead.

Envelopes transport your carefully contemplated and crafted words to your friends. Ensure you always include a return address to avoid these loyal messengers from a life in the abyss of postal limbo; left in an impersonal storage facility should their mission fail. Properly address them and they should attain their goal and yours too. We will address envelopes later.

Stamps

On the face of it, stamps play a decorative role. We might not realize that they have dual contrasting personalities. One side of their nature, akin to the traditional banker, demands prudent investments, a conservative approach as they accurately finance the expedition of your correspondence. The other side is that of the adventurous travel representative providing safe passage locally or across the globe via whatever possible route; their sovereignty acknowledged by each country's borders. Your letter has no guarantee of arriving safely without their authority or financial backing.

Purchase the 'forever' stamps to avoid the inconvenience of having to add additional postage whenever there is a price change. You will need the appropriate international stamps for letters going abroad. You may also have to pay extra for letters exceeding specific sizes or weight. Always consult the seller if you are unsure.

Recent years have seen an increase in the availability of themed stamps which, when chosen wisely, enhance the envelope and your letter as a whole. Visit your post office, authorized seller, or purchase online to see what options are available.

Never deface a stamp. Strict rules are in place regarding this so do not attract any trouble and simply stick your stamp(s) on the envelope as required. Always best to keep everyone happy.

Address Book

In general, you will post your letters to your friends. Addresses are easy to forget and therefore an address book is most useful in keeping this vital information. Use a notebook initially if you prefer but remember to index it by writing each letter of the alphabet at the top of the pages to help you find the correct information.

One noteworthy point; keep a copy of your address book in case you lose it. You could type the names, addresses and other contact information into your computer and print it off. This is just as effective as having an address book. Again, the choice is entirely yours; do what works best for you.

Words for Letters

Notebook and Pencil

An absolute must have! Carry a handy sized notebook and pencil for jotting notes, ideas, or reminders regarding your friends. Perhaps you might create a section to dedicate a page or two per month to write small reminders of occasions such as anniversaries, graduations, birthdays etc., or any other special dates which may warrant a letter. Recording when you sent and received letters is also useful. Every now and again we all let the odd things slip away, we are busy with other day-to-day matters and, before you know it, a few weeks have slipped by. In reverse, if you have sent a letter to your friend and not received a reply for a while, contact them and ask if they have received your letter because it may not have reached them.

Have you ever had a bright idea and then forgotten it? It happens to all of us. Your notebook will be there to the rescue! Jot ideas, thoughts, experiences, and feelings about events you have attended, places visited, activities, and anything else that attracts your attention. You may see a poster or advertisement which you know your friend will be interested in. If you travel by train or bus regularly you will see many advertisements on boards, in newspapers and magazines or hear other people discussing a film, show or other social activity. You may know a friend who would like to do the same or maybe you see an event and would like a friend to accompany you. Write a few notes to start your plan of how you will persuade your friends to join you. A letter of invitation is now in the offing.

Certain types of letters require a very careful approach. Preparation is the key for these sorts of correspondence and the earlier you start the more likely you will find the right words. Dedicate a section in your notebook for this purpose. You can scribble notes on how you may want to handle a delicate situation. If you change your mind about what you want to say add the words below your initial thoughts. Never cross out your thoughts because you never know if these will be useful when writing on a separate occasion to another friend in a similar situation. Think of this as 'thought investment' which will pay dividends when you occasionally review your notebook.

Scrap Paper

You gain environmental points and are acting smart when you use scrap paper. Moments of complete brain freeze have a recurring habit. The words lodged firmly in your pen rebuff every enticement to leave. The page waits and waits. Nothing appears. All is quiet. Palpable activity diminishes to sighs and pensive chin stroking. Windows are stared through. The pen remains adamant that not one word will reach the nib or beyond.

You may think this only happens to you - wrong! Every person I know who writes letters experiences this void more than once. Some go for a short walk, others go and make tea or coffee hoping this will somehow extricate the desired words. Prior to acknowledging an impasse, scribble down roughly what you want to say on the scrap paper, play with it, move this here and that there, doodle, or whatever it takes to restart the words landing on the page. Should your endeavors fail to reestablish your creative flow, tidy up the scrap paper and save it; you will need to read your thoughts again later. This is simply not your day. Accept it. Tomorrow will be different and you will regroup your thoughts and resume with a fresh mind.

Scrap paper is also useful when refilling your fountain pen or changing the cartridge. Once the operation is complete, write a few words or let your inner artist create a few swirls to ensure the ink is flowing smoothly before continuing writing. An even flow makes a better impression.

Another use for scrap paper is to practice any drawings you may want to include in your letter, no matter how simple. Add fun by including little sketches into your letters but keep them appropriate to the tone. A simple illustration or decoration introduces a different personal touch. However, do not overdo this or your friend will lose track of your thoughts and the letter's purpose becomes unclear.

Blotting paper

Blotting is useful when using a fountain pen and dealing with spillage. You can use an absorbent paper towel too, which will do the job nicely.

Blotting paper is also used to make sure your ink has dried. Placing it onto your writing once you have finished will absorb any excessive ink. In general, the quality of pens, paper and ink normally prevents this from happening but if you do experience it you now know how to resolve it.

Ruler

Rulers have been brought up on the straight and narrow, lead a simple life, and know where to draw the line. You will need their help to write on plain paper. Whether you use lined or plain paper is your choice. Those of you whose predisposition align with meticulously straight rows and plumb-line perfect margins and yet, at the same time, are attracted to structure free plain paper, fear not. Your straight-edged companion serves to resolve this paradox.

The under-sheet is one of life's bare essentials for the framework fanatics. Make your own customized under-sheets in several sizes; do a good job on this and enjoy your rewards over and over. The first task involves selecting one of your sheets of paper, preferably one for each size of paper you have neatly filed in your shoebox. Now, using your ruler measure down each side of your page and pencil in dots at the depth of line you feel matches the size of your writing and allows a little light between each line. Take a pen with a strong color (I suggest black) and draw lines across the page. Select the margin size you would like and draw a vertical line on each side of the page at your desired margin width. Do this for each size of paper in your stockpile. Create more than one for each size. You have now successfully created your under-sheet.

Next, take a piece of your writing paper and place it over the under-sheet; you need to see the lines you have drawn on the under-sheet through the writing paper. Congratulations. You now have the means to write in straight lines on plain paper. A simple but useful technique visually enhances your writing.

Your under-sheet will look similar to this:

Experiment with different options. Some layouts are more suitable to certain types of letters than others. Always consider your reader first; you may have to write a little larger than normal if your recipient has difficulty reading without glasses. Small children will read your writing much more easily if you make your handwriting bigger or maybe even write in capital letters.

The Shoebox

Would you consider the shoebox as the most valuable object on our planet? Never abandon a shoebox; you will not regret it. You have a wonderful container to save your pens, inks, writing paper, envelopes, stamps, address book, scrap paper, blotting paper, ruler, and anything else you wish to store away in your correspondence chest. As a side note, (and depending on how you view life) upon purchasing a shoebox, a free pair of shoes is included. Pick one containing an elegant and comfortable pair. Clearly, a shoebox has more than one sole purpose.

You may experience your uncontrollable artistic flair yearning to embellish your delectable depository. Give this urge full reign and lovingly adorn it. Decorative transformation is all part of the fun and creativity. Please do not hide it away on a remote and seldom visited shelf but instead give it pride of place in your sanctuary as a constant reminder of your connection with your friends.

Shoeboxes have a pack mentality; they serve you better in numbers. I recommend you acquire more. You already have one to stash your materials; perhaps use an additional one to keep letters awaiting reply and another to archive those which have been answered. The two additional boxes will help keep you organized and up-to-date with your correspondence. Letters have the remarkable quality of being enjoyed time and time again. When we think about our friends we can re-read their letters and still capture the feeling of their presence. The sense of touch from holding the letter heightens how we feel about the words on the paper.

In years and generations to come your archive of letters will interest your children, grandchildren, and beyond. Your archive is a legacy for those who come after you and paints the picture of your life in all sorts of hues. Imagine how you would connect with the generations that follow you. The words will pass through the decades to reach them. A tangible testimony showing the kind of person you and your friends were, sharing your thoughts, happiness, sadness, and your day-to-day life. A handwritten record forged by their ancestors.

Assembling Your Collection

Remember earlier, I let slip you can put all this together for possibly zero cost and could magically maintain this level of expenditure? Draw the curtains, glance over your shoulder, and quietly close the door. Be sure you are not being spied upon. The secret is about to be revealed to you.

Words for Letters

Assemble your own raiding party by summoning everyone living in your house together. Light the beacons, call in the banners to amass trusted friends and others who have sworn allegiance to you. Order them to ransack your house by rooting through all the drawers; especially the drawer nobody ever talks about, where forgotten keys, old membership cards, half used candles, and single shoelaces meditate and enjoy the gentler pace and tranquility of their existence. Your marauders must leave no stone – or cushion – unturned. If you live on your own, search incognito, think of it as an undercover mission. This opening forage will yield scrap paper, an assortment of ballpoints, pencils, a few envelopes, and possibly a stamp or two. Target your printer for a few sheets of paper for your first letter. Keep the plunder to yourself. Of course you can let your fellow looters keep any other bits of unrelated finds to reward their loyalty. Throw a celebratory banquet and dismiss your freebooters back to whence they came. Fortune may have smiled and you have already discovered a shoe box for your haul but if not find something else as a temporary repository until the right opportunity comes along. Congratulations! Your pillaging phase is finished.

You now turn to negotiation; the heart of the secret. Be guided by the spirits of the great Roman orators and matriarchs as you persuade and influence others in this negotiation process. However, only wear the toga and other investiture related garbs in your imagination; we do not want you to catch a cold or be seen to have lost the plot at such a crucial stage.

Remember those wonderful birthday and other special day gifts you received for years and stored at the back of the closet? You know, the gifts you annually consolidate into a large black plastic bag, tighten the drawstrings, and secretly tuck away into the shadowy recesses of your attic – not so much a hoard-away but more of a hideaway. After all, nobody needs an ever-increasing mountain of socks, hideous sweaters, cheap bath soap, and scent akin to paint stripper.

Put a stop to all this immediately! This is the new you! Liberate your stockpile and donate to thrift shops and companies who specialize in industrial paint stripping. Draw up a list of all those people who have misjudged your taste in clothing and cosmetics. Divide them into groups by family, proximity, or other criteria. Be sure not to miss anyone or you will incur further covert trips up into the attic.

Prepare and steel yourself for addressing each listed group of gift bearers. The time has come. You must proclaim loudly that you no longer wish to receive such time-proven gifts. Make it clear your appreciation will heighten and gratitude abound if they bought and brought pens, inks, assortments of paper, envelopes, or a book of stamps for you on gifting occasions.

The cat is now among the pigeons. The fox has entered the hen house. The word spreads. News of your rebellion proliferates betwixt your friends. Your pennants fly defiantly on the wind, gasps of astonishment ensue and headshaking is rife. A perfect moment for you to strike. Compose your letters immediately and give wings to your words; swooping into doubters' mailboxes. Spread the message! Skeptical hands warily open envelopes, eyes travel your lines, grimacing faces relax and begin to shine like the sunrise on midsummer's day. The slight ripple of a smile, a seat takes the weight, a re-read. The sun rises a little higher and the smile broadens. Oh joy of joys! You have them. You have touched their heart and spirit. Now, ask for whatever you want; your shoebox will prosper plenty-fold. Enjoy your triumph as a world of rediscovered kinship emerges. A world not built on speed and convenience but with roots entrenched firmly in consideration and devotion in friendship. A world which cares far beyond the tickle of a keyboard or a finger swipe.

I suspect there are those who may judge this a trifle over the top, but not everyone enjoys a full sense of appreciation.

Before our euphoric feelings sweep us away, we must steady ourselves and feel the firm ground beneath our feet and apply ourselves to another practicality.

Words for Letters
Handwriting
Fully paid-up members of the Shabby Scrawlers Society fear that their scribble is hopelessly indecipherable and avert the risk of humiliation by using a keyboard. Such a pity, nevertheless understandable. Good news! You can improve your chirographical expertise - I was going to add 'beyond recognition' but that is too ironic. Instead, let's say improve immensely with just a little practice.

Letters from one of my closest friends always look like ants carrying small leaking tins of black paint have meandered around a furrowed field in the snow, but he always writes a fabulous letter. Yes, his writing is awful, but would I want to miss any chance of receiving one of his hilarious letters? Definitely not! So, thankfully he has never let his lack of handwriting skills get in the way.

With a little practice your handwriting will excel. Remember the scrap paper you amassed from your earlier plundering? Keep your stockpile fed regularly. Pick out the lined sheets; if there are none, place plain scrap paper onto one of the under-sheets you created. Start by writing a series of letter 'o's. *Top tip:* take your time. Quality always outshines quantity. Keep in mind you write a letter at your own pace, not anyone else's, carry that thought into your handwriting practice. Try a few lines of 'c's. Feeling adventurous? Tackle a few rows of 'r's. Think of the top of the 'r' as the first leaf on a very young plant. Moving on even further practice 'b's and 'd's. Oh, and as the saying goes: mind your ps and qs.

Exercise your pen by slowly repeating other letters. Take control of the pen and let it do its job, you are just the driver. Form short words and then progress to longer ones or small phrases. Never let your handwriting stop you from creating enjoyable letters which your friends will love to read. Keep in mind one indisputable and vital fact. Your sentiments, thoughts, feelings and wishes create the magic, not your scrawl.

Many books and websites can help you improve your handwriting. Please do not become hung up on any misgivings you have about yours. It is all part of the fun.

Chapter 3

Basic Letter Layout

We have it in our power to begin the world over again.
~ Thomas Paine ~

Are you ready to start? We are about to explore the simple layout of a letter. Most of the letters we write will use this format. A structure simplifies writing your letter and helps us to connect more easily with our reader;  otherwise the task may appear rather daunting. Here goes! Is your pen hovering? Is your excitement bordering on the frenzied? Hold on tight!

Wait! Hold the horses! Before we gallop off, racing through the write-this-here-write-that-there phase, I should explain to you that we will cover both the U.S. and U.K way of writing an address. You never know when you will need this vital knowledge.

Oh, and the date format is different too, so we best cover that and then see how they all fit together. We are going to start with the letter.

Some people include their name on the first line. Others dismiss this as unnecessary because you identify yourself later. Where letters are more formal I suggest you include your name, but on personal letters to close friends you can omit it without causing major offence or breaking too many rules.

The U.S. Address

Write your address in the top right corner. The address you write should be the one where you would like your reply sent to. Only include the country in cases of international correspondence.

>123 Street,
>City, State, Zip code
>U.S.A (optional)

The U.K. Address

Write your address in the top right corner. The address you write should be the one you would like your reply sent to. As above, the country is only necessary for international correspondence.

>123, Street name,
>Area (optional)
>Town or City,
>Post code.
>Country (optional)

The Date

The date is important. Your friend should know when you wrote the letter. In addition, one day when your friends look back through their letters the date will help remind them of when you wrote the letter and what was happening in their life at that time. Dating the letter also helps to keep correspondence in order. We have a chronological recorded communication and can see how relationships have developed and occasions came and went.

Words for Letters

Leave a blank line, add the date. Choose the format of the date you would like to use. The samples throughout this book use either the UK format which is the day ordinal number (1^{st,} 2nd 3rd etc.) followed by the month and year or the US format; month first with nominal number, (1 2 3 etc.) comma, then the year.

The U.K. address and date

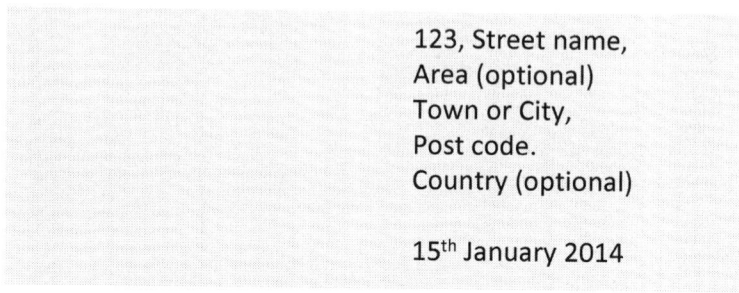

The U.S. address and date

We can now put behind us the international differences for a short while and our pens can continue forth as one body united in the common interest of caring for our friends.

The Salutation

Next is the salutation. Always include this. Leave a blank line before the salutation. You are not only greeting your friend but accurately stating whom you are writing to. In instances where you include more than one letter in the same envelope, the salutation helps clarify which person should read it. Use the person's name, nickname, or whatever you wish as long as it clearly identifies the recipient.

Include a comma after your salutation.

> 123, Street name,
> Area (optional)
> Town or City,
> Post code.
> Country (optional)
>
> 15th January 2014

Dear Anne,

The Body

The body of your letter follows the salutation. Regard it as telling a story. Do you recall the three parts of a story you were taught at school? Well, that works here too and goes along the old trusted lines of:

- ❖ Say what you are going to say.
- ❖ Say it.
- ❖ Say what you have said.

Stick with this; it is time proven, easy to write and easy to read. Indent your paragraphs to help visually break up the different points you make.

Say what you are going to say. Start with a good opening line that captures your friend's attention and signals what your letter is about, thus easing your friend into the letter and indicating what is to follow. Try to avoid a dull or clichéd opening. Capture their attention. Your relationship with your friend is unique and special; make your letter just as unique and special too.

> Dear Anne,
>
> You had better sit down to read this. I want to tell you about something which will have you dancing for joy. You won't believe what I found out earlier today, and before I go any further you need to know I expect your full support on this

Anne will read the above opening and feel excitement for what is to follow. The writer clearly wants to tell her about something which will be the letter's focal point but has deliberately held back any details. Anne has also been told how she will react to this and has been asked to take a blind leap of faith in supporting her friend. Whatever this is, her friend's enthusiasm will cause Anne to feel both curious and excited.

The opening promises an exciting letter, it already has an upbeat feel to it. She has to read on to discover what has caused her friend to write to her in this way.

Say it. Keep your letter focused by following an outline, more on outlines later. Make sure you keep the tone appropriate to the purpose. Your story unfolds throughout this phase. Avoid negativity in your story. Such thoughts may portray you as a whiner; your friend may disagree with you or feel less inclined to reply. Perhaps ask for an opinion, or ideas relating to your topic. Your friend will feel more engaged, and you are helping them with how to reply to you. Although you may be telling your friend your news try to include other people in the letter or drop in comments like 'you would have laughed so much' or 'We had to drag Paul and Mark away'. Try to paint an image in your reader's mind to keep your letter interesting.

The letter continues:

> Dave, Jo, Nic, and I met for lunch down by the park – they all say hi and hope you like your new job. Jo has been busy checking out weekend activity breaks. One event jumped off the page at her: a weekend of archery for beginners! Imagine that! How many times have we talked about doing something new like that?
>
> The course runs the last weekend in March. It starts early on Saturday morning and finishes at 4pm on the Sunday. We could travel up on the Friday evening and return Sunday night. You must come and give it a go! I doubt we will be Robin Hood standard but we do get to try different types of archery. It's a very reasonable price too. There is a hotel close by.
>
> Dave cannot make it – he's away that whole week but Jo and Nic are up for it. You must come. You have plenty of time to free up your busy calendar. I asked Jo to send all of us the details, so keep an eye out for that.
>
> We can all travel together. Nic has kindly offered to drive if we all meet at his house.

The letter, in effect, is an invitation. It brims with enthusiasm and makes Anne feel special. Her friends have discovered an event, thought of her, and invited her to join them.

Say what you have said. You are approaching the end of your letter. This part should tie up very closely with your opening. You are moving your reader to the close. A short paragraph does the job nicely for you. If you are asking your friend to do something for you then this is a good place to succinctly ask or repeat your request thus leaving your friend a clear reminder of what you are asking them to do.

Anne's friend goes on to say:

> Anne, we cannot miss this. I expect you will be dancing up and down now. When you have calmed down drop me a line to tell me you are coming. This will be so much fun!!!!

The letter's high energy keeps going and her friend has asked Anne for another commitment by requesting her to confirm her attendance. The letter writer has told Anne what to do next.

The Closing

The closing does exactly what is says. It closes the letter. Leave a blank line after the body and add the closing. What do you say? Numerous options are available here but if you are completely stumped then a plain 'Yours,' is adequate. Place a comma after your chosen closing. Try to make the closing a reflection of both your friendship and the tone of your letter. Be inventive. See what springs to mind.

Leave a blank line after the closing.

Back to Anne's letter:

> Your brother in arms,

A nice little close which reflects both the content and tone of the letter.

The Signature

Sign here! Yes, time to identify yourself! Sign your name appropriately to both the letter and to the person to whom you wrote. Use your full name, first name, a nickname, or even a name which complements the tone, purpose, and theme of the letter.

The Post Script

You are all done. Wait a minute. Oh no! You left something out! Perhaps you want to add a detail you forgot, or a thought which just popped into your head. Relax, this happens. The Post Script is on hand to rescue the situation. Simply start a new line after the signature with 'P.S.' and add your extra words. The P.S. signals to your friend that you wish to add to the body of the letter. Phew! That was close.

In the letter to Anne we might see:

P.S. The hotel we hope to stay at has a pool and sauna so pack your swimsuit!

The Enclosure

Suppose you want to include an item such as a photograph or newspaper cutting, in which case, you should inform your friend you have done so. The item may have already been referenced in the body of the letter, but be safe rather than sorry. Your photograph may be discarded unknowingly because the recipient did not see it inside of the envelope.

To declare items included with your letter start a new line after the signature (or P.S.) with 'Enc:'. This is an abbreviation for Enclosures. Jot down how many there are or list them. The Enc: option is useful because it acts as a reminder to actually put the enclosures into the envelope with your letter and avoid an awkward oops moment. You would not be the first to miss including an enclosure, some of us, have done this more than once.

Mistakes

Modern science fully acknowledges migrant gremlins squat inside of your pen and cause mistakes to occur. Luckily they do not stay long and move on. They lure you to write the wrong word or phrase. Rather than attack the word or phrase with a frenzied pen, draw a neat line through the error and continue calmly.

Top tip: Wider margins allow you to include words or phrases and indicate where they belong by drawing an arrow to where you want them to be read.

Only if your page starts to look like a capital city's metro map should you consider rewriting the whole page or letter.

The Envelope

Coordinated envelopes and writing paper add class to your letter. Birthday and other gifting days boost your collection with varying colors and sizes. Your letters portray you; your personal ambassadors carrying the responsibility to represent you. A reader's first impressions matter. Make them count by taking that little extra effort to show how much you care.

One practice you might wish to follow is to address the envelope before you write your letter to help you visualize your recipient. Having a photograph or memento helps too. Writing his or her name and address actively encourages images of your friend in your mind's eye and helps to compose a more personal correspondence.

Equip your envelope with the correct information to prevent any mishaps along the way. Write clearly. Begin with the person's name and follow with the address.

We are dealing with addresses once more so we must observe international standards. Only include the country if your letter is to go abroad.

U.S. Addressed Envelope

Name,
Street Address,
City, State, Zip code.
Country (optional)

U.K. Addressed Envelope – Block Style

The example below is in block style; all the information is vertically aligned.

>Name,
>House name, (optional)
>Street Address,
>Town or City,
> County (optional)
> Post Code
> Country (optional)

U.K. Addressed Envelope Indented Style

Alternatively you may use an indented style. Either will suffice.

>Name,
> House name, (optional)
> Street Address,
> Town or City,
> County (optional)
> Post Code
> Country (optional)

What happens to your letter if you incorrectly address it? Suppose your friend has moved and not told you. Perhaps there are other problems or difficulties in play to prevent your letter from reaching its intended destination.

Always include a return address on your envelope to assist in the event of your letter experiencing delivery complications. The U.S. and the U.K have differing practices on where to write the return address.

U.S. Return Address

In the USA this is written in the top left corner. Be mindful to keep your return address small to eliminate any confusion with the intended destination. This example shows a typical layout for an envelope using domestic addresses.

Your Street Address,
City, State, Zip code

Name,
Street Address,
City, State, Zip code

In the U.K. the standard practice is to write the return address on the back of the envelope. Do not include the country if the letter is domestic rather than international.

If undelivered please return to:

Your Street Address, Town, Post Code

The Stamp

Affix your stamp into the top right corner. Always ensure the correct amount for the stamp to avoid embarrassment to both you and your friend.

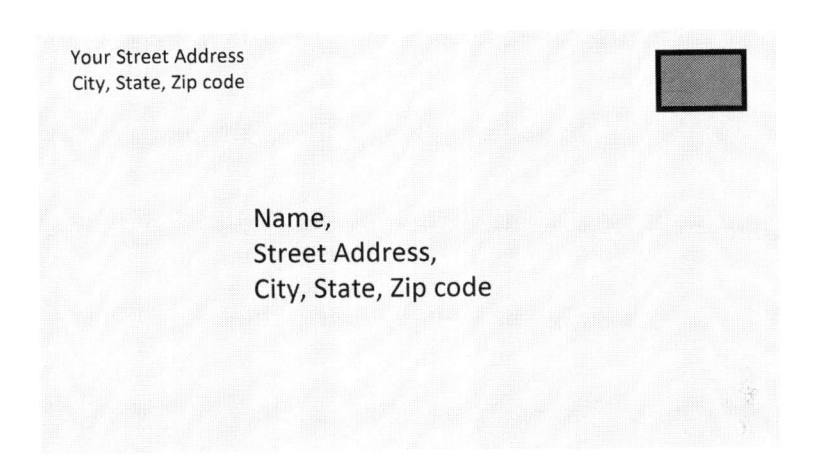

```
Your Street Address
City, State, Zip code


                    Name,
                    Street Address,
                    City, State, Zip code
```

Place your written letter in the envelope. *Top Tip:* Place the letter fold to the bottom of the envelope to prevent from accidentally being sliced in half by a letter opener.

One final reminder, please make double sure you have inserted any enclosures.

Part 2

Chapter 4

Letters are more than just Words

Let us become the change we seek in this world.
~ Mohandas Karamchand Gandhi~

Words alone cannot express how important the gifts of friendship and love are, but *words together* can. Words can fill pages but pages full of considered and thoughtful words can fill hearts and change lives.

Mary's grandma sips her tea and worries. Has Mary settled in at her university? Is she safe? Has she made any friends? Grandpa would have been so proud. Footsteps outside, her cup lowers. Ah, the mailman. A pink envelope nestles in her mailbox. Butterflies rise and flap elatedly through her entire body. She recognizes the lettering. A deep breath – Oh Mary you are safe! She smiles.

We delight in connecting with our loved ones. The joy of sharing happy times together whether through meeting, chatting, attending parties, giving and receiving gifts, or just watching a movie huddled together on the couch warms our lives. We also bond in other ways by giving support and comfort to each other on those days when dark clouds block the sun's warmth.

Perhaps on occasion face-to-face contact with those we love evades us. Isolation is rarely pleasant but you can connect in other ways by telephone call, text, social media, a note or a letter. In the above scenario Mary connects to her grandma via a letter to show her she cares. Her grandma feels that connection from the moment she receives the letter, yes, even before she opens it.

Special Connection

We touched earlier on why you might send a letter instead of calling or using social media. Each method communicates but a handwritten letter brings people together in a unique and special way; it bonds them through calling upon more of the senses. As Mary's grandma holds the envelope she can *feel* the texture. She can *see* her granddaughter's handwriting, maybe even *smell* her scent. With all this sensory activity before she opens the envelope, her anxiety over Mary transforms to excitement and relief.

We leave Mary's grandma to read her letter in private. Consider what she might do with it. I wonder how many times she will read it. No doubt Mary's letter will stay close to her, but as Mary writes more, Grandma will save her letters with Mary's other mementos as a reminder of her granddaughter and maintain their closeness in Mary's absence. She might see it as a milestone or family heirloom, a record of Mary's first impressions of university life. The letter still has value after it has been read. Yes, it has fulfilled the first role of communication but then other qualities come into play. The dynamics change as each subsequent letter deepens the relationship between the two.

Your letter is a gift to your friends adding a smile to their faces or perhaps offering comfort. Likewise, when you receive one, your life will be touched in some small part. By staying connected to our family and friends, we not only maintain our relationships, but we give them a future; so much more than a simple communication. Letter writing calls for a little extra time and effort to connect personally. The time is well spent and the effort well directed. You will enjoy many happy years ahead.

Consideration

The previous chapter dealt with the physical aspects of layout. This chapter covers the approach to writing your letter. The remainder of Part 2 contains samples of types of letters you may wish to create and suggests ways to go about writing them.

Writing a letter can become almost ritualistic. After all, you are setting some time aside to focus on someone you care for. Unless exigent circumstances dictate, there is no point in frenetically scribbling and dispatching it immediately. Take your time. Think of a letter as a hug with words. You would not want to rush that now would you? Because if you did, it would not be a hug would it?

Prior to starting we ought to clear up a couple of sticking points which cause people to freeze or halt in their tracks before they even start. Fear leaps in and takes over, crushing their will to write. Think about that for a moment. The fear has stopped a personal connection between two friends. Why? Well, some people are afraid of writing to people because they lack confidence in their spelling and/or grammar. They worry about what others may think. They do not want to feel humiliated so they take the protective option, retreat into their shell and the shoebox is tidied away for another time. So, we shall deal with this right now.

Spelling and grammar are 'technical issues' so treat them as such. Never allow a technical issue to stop you from writing a letter to those you love and care for. Never. Never. Never. One day you might regret missing out on an opportunity to deepen your friendships.

Spelling: The more you practice the better you become. Keep your laptop or equivalent device handy and check any spellings using the word processor or online dictionary. Use a good old fashioned printed dictionary if you have one. Being told to look up a word you cannot spell in the dictionary does carry a flaw in the logic; if you cannot spell it how can you look it up? What chance have you got with words like pneumonia? We should strive to spell words correctly, but if we make a mistake so what? Will the world stop spinning? Do not ignore your friends by using spelling as a reason to fail to connect with them in such a special way. Your friends are not interested in evaluating your spelling skills but in your message, your thoughts, your warmth, and your consideration. Point out to anyone who does comment on spelling mistakes that you are amazed that they can only spell a word one way! As someone wrote in a letter to me recently, 'the spell checker in my pen has stopped working, so be grateful for the entertainment in deciphering this'. Priceless! Mind you, English speaking countries have many variations for spelling words so perhaps claim ancestry to one of the more exotic islands.

Grammar: Secret grammar police are everywhere and ever vigilant to seize a chance to display their knowledge. Ignore them. Like spelling, grammar has a place in providing a structure for you to communicate, but it should not stop you from writing. We all make mistakes. Writing and making mistakes is far more important than not writing at all. Practice does improve your grammar. Deliberately breaking the rules of grammar can be so much fun too!

Another fear we should deal with relates to beginners fearing their vocabulary is too limited and fearing the struggle to find the right word. That happens to everyone. However, here is another secret to be kept strictly between us: if you are really stuck and struggling to find the word you want, just make one up! Did you spot the words I made up while writing this book? And besides, the word you make up might catch on. Language is ever-changing; words come and go. The main point to letter writing is showing someone you care and you are prepared to make an effort for them. Your message outshines any technical issues with the way you express your care for others.

Preparation and Composition

The steps below will help you to write your first personal letter. Read them, think about each one and try them out a few times to see how well they work for you. It is impossible to write one process for all people in all circumstances. Feel free to change them to suit your particular situation.

Words for Letters

Warning: Never write a letter in anger. The chances are that you will regret it in the future. However, if you do write a letter when angry resist the urge to post it. Once it goes you cannot stop it! Leave it for a day or two, re-read it and think how you might rewrite this in a more positive tone.

Is your pen poised over your writing paper? Stop right there. Put it down. Pick up your pencil and scrap paper. We have to do a little preparatory work first.

- Choose someone to write to.
- Think about this person. Picture them in your mind.
- Decide on the purpose of your letter. Select the letter type: congratulations, thank you, condolence, or simply a letter to keep in touch.
- Contemplate on how you want the person to feel when they read it.
- Will you enclose a photograph, a newspaper cutting, or other relevant item? Make sure the item is suitable for posting and is close at hand.
- Jot down topics or phrases you would like to include. Do they match your letter's purpose? Take your time.
- How would you like the person to reply to your letter?
- Start a draft outline of your letter on scrap paper with a few simple headings.
- Think about the tone of your letter. What mood do you wish to create?
- Review your topics and phrases. Which would you include? Strike out the others.
- Produce your first draft on scrap paper. Keep in mind the three parts and work on each section to create a smooth flow.
  - The opening
  - The main body
  - The closing
- Leave it for a while – preferably overnight. It always helps to look at things with fresh eyes.
- Review your draft and make any changes you need.

- ❖ Consider which stationery and ink to use. Will the size, style and color be harmonious with your letter's tone?
- ❖ Write your letter based on your reviewed draft; change it as you see fit.
- ❖ Do not forget to include any enclosures.

Where and When to Write

Upon entering this world, your pen will cascade correspondence and radiate warmth on whomever you deem worthy. You no longer need your job, all tedious tasks take flight, and monotonous moments melt away. Your life metamorphoses from routine to a bird soaring and gliding carefree between sunbeams whenever and wherever you choose. Everything and everywhere is bathed in happiness and contentment.

If only this were true.

You know it is not. What a shame; I almost believed it myself for a minute. Never mind; it's back to earth to set out with determination to find ways to deepen our friendships.

Your day-to-day schedule influences your opportunities to write. Examine your routine to unlock the shackles of drudgery and discover precious moments of freedom to ply pen to paper.

Jot down your typical weekly activity on scrap paper. A few weeks will differ because of holidays and special one-time activities. Focus your attention on what you would regard as an average week; search out a couple of openings you could dedicate to personal correspondence. Do you lean toward a couple of hours on an evening at a desk or table with the mandatory cup of tea and supporting scone, cake or chocolate of your choice? Self-indulgence in the simple pleasures of life is just reward for your commitment to changing the world for the better.

Commuting on public transport presents regular possibilities. A shaky train or bus journey apart from shuffling your bones around, offers chances to introduce ideas into your notebook. Perhaps lunchtime peregrinations may lead you to your preferred nook to contemplate further inspirations, plans or even plots.

Even a few minutes consideration can yield thoughts rich in possibilities and lay the foundations for further exploration. Capture their essence immediately, otherwise they vanish. Once planted, ideas can only grow. One of your brain's great assets is the ability to create or receive ideas. Use it!

Creatures of habit like to write letters from the same place and at the same time of day or night. Free spirits prefer more variety in their approach. No rules are in place; go with whatever works for you. Committing to writing regularly helps establish good habits and yields frequent self-rewards. How often you write to someone depends on the other person's commitment too. Once you start writing to people and they reply, the rest tends to take care of itself. You soon begin to spot opportunities to raise the shoebox lid.

Give it a go!

You may be nervous about starting out. No bigger warehouse has ever or will ever be built to hold doubts about yourself than your own mind. We tend to be a little over-critical of our own abilities when we are nervous; especially when we are about to tackle something new. We worry so much that we fail to see the tremendous value of what we can give to others.

This is perfectly understandable and everyone experiences doubts. Others will respect you all the more if you give it a go. They will follow in your footsteps. You are creating a new level of connection and giving others the chance to share. You will be appreciated more than you think.

Food for Thought

Think of it like this; supposing a friend drops by unexpectedly on a cold and miserable day. You offer them coffee or tea and perhaps a warm scone. Easy. Right? You turn the oven or microwave on and pop the scone in long enough to warm it up. Meanwhile you boil the kettle and make two cups of tea (teapot optional depending on your taste.) Preparations finished, you serve warm scones with butter and possibly jam. Your friend enjoys the warmth of the food and tea on such a cold day. Do you think your friend is worried about exactly what heat you set the microwave on? Are you interrogated about the scone's composition; the butter's origin; where the tea was grown; and what logistics company delivered the goods to the shops? No you are not. Your friend is happy you shared warm food and tea, and that you sat together as friends chatting. The essence of the above connection lives not in the physical details but in the welcome and sharing.

So it is with your letter writing. Focus on the message and what you want to share not on the nuts and bolts of handwriting, grammar, syntax, or spelling.

The following chapters discuss several letter types. A chapter is dedicated to each letter type. There are other types of letters, but we want to cover enough to get you up and running – or in this case writing. These are not rules, just helpful suggestions. You know your friends and the circumstances, so you are the final judge on what is appropriate or not.

I have tried to keep the format similar for each chapter with the intention of developing a common approach to the different types of letters offered.

Chapter 5

A Letter of Congratulations

The only way to discover the limits of the possible is to go beyond them into the impossible.
~ Arthur C. Clarke ~

Stories of friends' achievements and successes uplift our hearts and inspire us towards our own goals. But suppose, that given our good intention, our felicitations have an equal chance of delighting or upsetting our successful achievers? Well, that takes the wind out of everyone's sails, doesn't it?

In this chapter we look at how we might avoid offending our friends on their triumphant days by acknowledging the successful fullfillment of one of their goals.

General Comment

All over the world people strive to meet their goals. Their aims may be personal and set by themselves such as weight loss, fitness, or they may be defined by others for example at work, school, or as part of a sport or other activity. Some goals are met; some not. A portion may be achieved through struggles, others via a smoother route. Other peoples' successes warrant our attention.

Always send a letter of congratulations. You may have already verbally expressed your recognition and praise, but like our achievers, let us go the extra mile. Record their achievement by allowing your written words to follow your uttered tribute and mark a permanent testimony to stand witness forevermore. Casting these words in stone (pen to paper is more practical) enhances the experience for everyone and is your chance to capture a little piece of history. How can others' achievements inspire us if we ignore them or allow apathy to diminish their feats into eternal anonymity?

Stay Alert! Be permanently on the lookout for the chance to offer congratulations. Hone all your senses until you can smell the chances floating on the breeze. Yes, you can be that good. How do you know when and how to offer your praises?

It is easy! You hear about an accomplishment, a graduation for instance. You visit the local shop, head for the card section, scour for the Congratulations section, select a card, purchase it, write the recipient's name and a couple of words, scribble your own name, address the envelope, post it, and off it goes. Job done. Pat on the back, and off to bed with a newborn hope that you may be invited to the free-to-you celebratory meal at a charming restaurant or a quaint venue with a tasty buffet. Is that it?

That depends on you. If you are happy, then so be it. Please allow me to congratulate you on qualifying for membership in the Society of Advocates for Adequacy.

What is missing? Could you have done more? Look at how you might spot further opportunities and take a more personal approach.

Check your radar for *Events* and *Actions*.

Events

Consider these:
1. **Calendar entries:** Birthdays, Anniversaries etc., those dates you unerringly circle year in and year out. And if

they are not on your calendar start gathering the intel and record those dates!
2. **Achievements:** Single instances such as promotions, sports awards, and educational awards. Include group goals too, perhaps a target reached for a charity or a concert recital.
3. **Milestones:** Similar to both of the above but attract a broader recognition such as a Silver Wedding Anniversary, 100th birthday, or maybe a group reaching a membership goal or marker.

Each event is outwardly identifiable. Calendar or cyclic based events are easy to spot. Other related events are also easy to spot especially when you are interested and in touch with those involved. Keep your ear to the ground, listen in on conversations, and generally raise and expand your noseiness.

Actions

The words 'Unsung Heroes' relate to actions most aptly. Here we are concerned with a branch of humankind selflessly devoting their energies to other people or beneficial causes. May we not congratulate these admirable folk? Do you value virtues like perseverance, courage, curiosity, forgiveness, and kindness? Then surely, when fortune allows you to witness fellow humans undertaking such acts, you must congratulate them. Add your support and encouragement to these special hearts.

Worthy actions are easily missed. I urge you to be constantly seeking for these deserving, unsung heroes.

Approach

Preparation, as ever, is the key. Spend a little time thinking about:

- ❖ What exactly is the event or action?
- ❖ How are you connected to the occasion and the people involved? Be realistic. Be honest.

- How important this is to you?
- How much do you care?
- How important is it to others?
- When did it happen?
- Who was involved?

To help you put the event or action into context...

- **Look into the past:** Why did this happen? How did this situation start? How long has this been going on for?
- **Look at the present:** What has just happened or is it still in the process of happening? How are people affected by it? Who are the beneficiaries?
- **Look to the future:** What will this mean going forwards? What new hopes are there?

Think also about *what message you are sending?* How do you expect the recipient to react?

Regard a congratulatory letter as having four pillars. Before pen touches paper continue to reflect on how you will tell the person or group in your letter the following:

- **Notice:** You have noticed the acievement.
- **Recognition:** Their insight, effort, courage, etc., has been recognized. Highlight the important aspects.
- **Appreciation:** Who will appreciate their efforts or achievements?
- **Share:** You want to share in applauding *their* success.

Why is all this preparation important?

The more groundwork you do, the more honest, personally meaningful, and powerful your congratulatory words will be. You will touch their hearts and inspire them further.

Be mindful, when writing your letter to focus on the events and actions not solely on the person or group. Your intention is not to create a celebrity but to share your recognition and appreciation of their achievement. If you spotlight and dwell on the person then the letter has become fan mail.

Warning: At no point in the letter should you try to steal recognition for yourself. This is not your show! Whether you had a small part to play or not, steer clear of trying to creep in on the action. People will spot your slithering and regard your intention as tasteless and selfish. You might want to avoid using expressions like 'I always knew you could do it', 'I am proud of you'; In short, do not be a creep!

Base your letter's body structure on the list below.

- ❖ Identify the event or action and cite details. Draw attention to its significance.
- ❖ Put the event or action and the person or group into context. Include the recognition, appreciation, and aspirations for the future.
- ❖ Restate your congratulations (not word for word!) and close warmly

In each letter sample in Part 2 I have deliberately excluded the address from the top right corner as these are sample letters to illustrate the points made so far. We touched on this earlier. The date, however, is still included.

Congratulations Letter Sample 1

In this first sample the event is a milestone birthday. As well as wishing his grandma a happy 90th birthday, Jules mentions some of her attributes, refers to her gardening skills, and even tasks her to make lemonade! It is light, warm and personal.

14th October 2013

Dear Grandma,

If you can read this letter without your glasses just a few days or so from your 90th birthday - then scientists will want to know the secrets of your perfect eyesight!

HAPPY 90th BIRTHDAY GRANDMA!

Each decade has presented you with challenges which have always been met with grace, dignity, and determination – some of us would say obstinacy. You have shown all of us that a good, honest, and simple lifestyle is key to living a long and fulfilling life.

So many people are grateful for your gardening encouragements and advice (or bossiness ☺). It is certainly no coincidence that your street is the most beautiful and colorful of the neighborhood, and long may it continue to be so.

As you know, I cannot be there for your party but the rest of the family will be there. Everyone is excited to spend this day with you. Of course you will have to do some work. You will not get away without making your secret lemonade. Aunt Milly swears you put a drop of gin in it! Make sure Granddad makes you breakfast in bed.

Happy Birthday and Congratulations on filling our lives with so much sunshine for so many decades.

Love and hugs,
Jules

P.S. Of course, if you did need your glasses to read this I will have to cancel the scientists' visits.

Words for Letters

Congratulations Letter Sample 2

Sample 2 is a letter to a group of people and congratulates them on reaching a target in their charitable cause. The reference to the past gives us information about how well the group has done to achieve the target. The present acknowledges the feelings of two beneficiaries. The future looks bright and optimistic.

8th January 2014

Dear Meg, John, Cyn, and Bart,

Congratulations on achieving your Winter Goal of $10,000 after the sponsored hill walk on New Year's Day. This is such a splendid effort all round. Your third event of the program has already taken you past your target. Remember earlier in November when it looked impossible? What a turnaround! the training itself through the winter would have been daunting enough but to add the extra effort of asking people to part with their money required super human determination. But, you all did it!

Two senior citizens at the Drop-in shelter are so excited about the new equipment you can now install. They told us all about how this will improve the lives of less fortunate people. Good things are being said all over town about the shelter's accomplishments.

Well, you still have two events of your winter program to go. "The Sounds of the 60s" will attract many more and as for the cake show, we drool with high expectation if last year's event is anything to go by.

No doubt many other felicitations are flying your way. You have done something very special for the community. Well Done! Well Done!

Big Smiles,
Clive and Will

Congratulations Letter Sample 3

Here we see congratulations offered to Phillipa on her promotion. It is lighthearted but also acknowledges all the efforts she has put into her work.

24th January 2013

Dear Phillipa,

News has leaked out; you can hide it no longer. We have discovered all about your promotion. You must be thrilled!! Your mother told us (don't worry we untied her from the chair after we had drained her of all that info) you are transferring to the office right here in town. So not just a better job but less travel too! Win-Win all the way!

The last three years of combining a full-time job and three nights per week at college have paid off. Everyone here remarks on how you did well to keep going on such a tough schedule. Is there a limit to how many ends you can burn a candle?

Your employers have recognized the effort and commitment you put in to your new career to reward you with a new opportunity. We are all happy for you and confident that your hard work will continue to bring you further success.

Congratulations from all of us! Do come and see us as soon as you are back.

Yours always,

Dean, Teresa, Ginny, Stacey, and Joe.

(or as you used to call us – the headbangers at No.26!!!)

With all these congratulations flying everywhere you might expect a party to follow. Perhaps now might be a good time to move on to invitations.

Chapter 6

A Letter of Invitation

Nothing annoys people so much as not receiving invitations.
~ Oscar Wilde ~

Imagine sending your own personal ambassador to announce your parties! Picture the surprise on your friend's faces as your ambassador proclaims the details of your proposed celebration and a request to attend it. Quality invitations are the forerunner to a successful party. Naturally you expect your ambassador to communicate the correct details, promote your event as appealing, provide the appropriate level of supporting information, and ask for an answer from your invitees.

Reflections

Your invitation is your ambassador; it reflects you to your friends and acts as testimony to:
- ❖ The quality of effort you are making
- ❖ How much consideration you show
- ❖ How enthusiastic you are to have your friends there
- ❖ Your commitment to your own event's success

The word *party* in this chapter refers to any event where people will gather at your request to mark an occasion.

Your ambassador's message must be clear and set the tone for the party to follow. The same message can be sent to all invitees, or personalize a few for particular recipients. Your message must contain the crucial details of the party, additional information to help your guests, and possibly suggestions to some or all of your guests.

Once you have selected the date of your party, calculate when your invitations should be sent out and by which date you will need your replies returned. Typically, the smaller and more informal the party the less notice is necessary but with larger groups the complexity increases. Show consideration and respect by giving people the right amount of notice; not too long that they cannot commit nor too short that they may already have other commitments or cannot organize any necessary arrangements in time. Three weeks may be ideal for a private dinner party but at least three months may be needed for a wedding.

Choosing your Ambassador

The physical composition of the invitation is important and ought to fit in with the theme and tone of your party. If the proposed guest list is small an individual letter to each invitee is more personal. A larger group might influence you towards using a printed invitation and if possible try to choose one which has sufficient blank space to handwrite a few warm words. You may also wish to add enclosures such as a map, parking information, or other noteworthy comments. Plan how best to co-ordinate all the items to give your desired impression. Consider how each item's color, texture, and quality will complement your theme.

Be aware that a shoddy invitation with a disjointed message not only fails to appeal to the recipient but also may be perceived as a statement of what you think of your intended guest.

Your invitees may want to keep the invitation as a memento of the occasion, especially if it is a special one such as a milestone anniversary or other once-in-a-lifetime occurrence carrying high sentimental value. Your letter or card becomes a special keepsake by which your guests will remember the event.

Instructing your Ambassador

An invitation must contain accurate information. Missing or incorrect details cause confusion thus increasing your amount of preparatory efforts. What starts off as a pleasurable prospect degenerates into a burden. You will be besieged with questions from *all* of your invitees, not just one. Worse still, your guests turn up at the wrong time or venue. Oops!

Below are three categories of information to consider.

Crucial Information

Certain details are essential to all parties. Be clear and concise and avoid ambiguity. Each invitee must know:

- The purpose of the party
- The date
- The start time (and end time if required)
- The location
- Anything you expect your guests to bring
- Whom to reply to, how to reply, and by when

Keep all of the above information together
.

Additional Information

After the crucial information, include additional information about the party so your invitees gain a clearer picture of what you intend to happen. Examples are:

- A map highlighting the location
- The special theme of the party
- An outline of the program if your party has booked entertainers performing at specific times
- Travel and accommodation details
- Car parking availability

- ❖ Special access for wheelchairs etc.
- ❖ Dress code
- ❖ Special dietary information
- ❖ Whether your guests may bring friends or if the party has exclusivity such as ladies only

Include any other details which you think are helpful or more suitable to your party.

Suggestions

A good ambassador reduces the amount of time you spend on preparations for your party. This has to be good news! Include all the essential information and if appropriate add a few suggestions for your guests. You might propose a costume theme or even ask them to bring a surprise dessert matching the theme. Keep it simple and think how to make it easy for your guests to accept your suggestions. If you ask your guests to bring something, consider how easy or difficult this could be to transport.

Final Checklist

Once you have written and collated everything refrain from sending your ambassadors out immediately. Having gotten this far, avoid any simple mishaps by:

- ❖ Checking and double checking the spelling of names and addresses
- ❖ Making a list of what is to be included for each invitee. You might enclose a map for those not familiar with the area but not to those who live locally
- ❖ Asking someone to help you by reading your invitation to ensure everything you said would be there is there

The proof is in the pudding as the saying goes.

Invitation Letter Sample 1

26th November 2012

Dear Pete and Megan,

    We are inviting you to a dinner party at our house to celebrate the New Year. We realize you are planning to be away from 31st December, so we are bringing the celebrations forwards to Saturday 29th December at 7pm.

    Invitations are also going to Paul, Sam, Christine, Mark, Jo, and Ang – in other words the usual gang.

    Given the topics of conversation the last time we were all together it only seems fitting that everyone should attend in Victorian attire – or the nearest you can manage! No doubt Mark's top hat will make an appearance. Also, as befitting, we will have the party by candlelight only, and each person should prepare to play various Victorian parlor games.

    We are not sure how late the party will continue but you are welcome to stay over if you wish to.

    Please reply by Saturday 15th.

Yours-in-excited-expectation,
John and Ella xx

The above letter is ideal for just a few personal friends. There is only one letter shown here but additional invitations would be sent to the others names in the letter with slight variations.

Larger Groups

A larger number of guests usually require more planning and additional considerations. You may wish to keep it personal but simply do not have the time to handwrite each invitation. Practicality must come to the fore in such situations because you might never have met some of your guests!

Words for Letters

The following steps are intended to help you to organize your invitations to a larger party. Add more or change things around a little to suit your particular circumstances.

- ❖ Make a guest list using a spreadsheet or simply write them on a piece of paper.
- ❖ Add columns to the right. See later in this chapter.
- ❖ Capture all the crucial and repetitive information into one place to reduce the amount of work in preparing and sending the invitations. Search the Internet or visit stationers to find a suitable pre-printed card. If you cannot find what you want, either use your own computer or ask a friend if they will help you to design your own card. See the sample Invitation card below.
- ❖ Calculate the size color, and texture of card, paper and envelope you would need and order

Invitation Card Sample.

Joe's Graduation Party

To..

You are invited to celebrate Joe's Graduation
with his family and friends.
Date: Friday 12 July Time: 3-6pm
Location: The Ice Cream Palace

A magician will perform 4-5pm
A buffet is available: 3.30-5:30

We will be delighted to see you!

Ample car parking space available behind the Palace.

RSVP by 27 June to *address*

A nice touch would be to have a photograph of Joe in his graduation garb on the other side of this card. The card has all the essential information and some additional information. Extra information could be included on a separate sheet with a simple map, useful telephone numbers, disabled access points, and perhaps details of the buffet. Don't forget to ask if anyone has any special dietary requirements.

No doubt there will be guests you know and others not as well. On occasions such as these a wise move is to write to a very select few. A busy day is ahead and you will need their helping hands. Select your 'victims' and include a letter into their envelope along the lines of:

Invitation Letter Sample 2

15 June 2013

Dear Milly,

Think of this letter as the greatest test of our thirty years friendship! Yes, even a bigger test than the camping disaster of 1998! Nevertheless, I am excited.

I have enclosed an invitation to you all to Joe's graduation party. This may prove to be a bridge too far! If Joe's friends are like Joe then anything can happen!

Yes, I know you are thinking that I am well capable of keeping everything running smoothly, but maybe I am enjoying another of those senior moments. I should appreciate it if you would accept the lofty role of 'Gift Manager' and marshal the gift table to ensure tags stay attached and the cards occupy the same table.

I know I can trust you to perform this mission in a firm but covert manner! ☺

We must get together soon for coffee I would like your opinion on some ideas for the party.

Yours as always,

Marg xx

Words for Letters

The letter brings added warmth to the invitation and makes Milly already feel a key part of the graduation. Letters are your ways of adding that closeness to your relationship. They are most definitely a hug with words.

Although you may have used the printed card and not included a letter, please write the envelope by hand. Just printing a label and sticking it on the envelope presents your invitation as impersonal; it may be confused with junk mail!

Keep your guest list up to date. If you add a few columns to the right of the guests you can use headings such as those illustrated below.

Tracking your Guest List

Name	Map	Letter	Sent	Reply	Nos.	Spec diet?	TY
Sam and Ella	N	Y	Y				
Mark and Anthony	Y	N	Y	Y	2	N	
Milly & family	Y	Y	Y	Y	4	N	
Mary and Jean	N	N	Y	Y	0		

Of course you would expect the guest list to be longer and you might include a column for the addresses. The simple chart above helps to see what you have included, if you have sent the invitation, received a reply, the number of people coming per invitation, special dietary considerations, and finally the Thank You column. This last column will be used to track that a Thank You letter has been sent to thank each guest for attending and for any gifts they may have brought.

The invitations are done; the party is over; which brings us to our next chapter concerning gratitude.

Chapter 7

A Thank You Letter

Gratitude is the memory of the heart.
~ Jean Baptiste Massieu ~

Two words that could change the world: Thank You! Yes, this is true. Gratitude is the most powerful energy source on Earth. When people are grateful good things happen all around us. Special warmth enters our lives and surrounds us. Become a Thank You revolutionary and spread happiness and contentment..

The landscape of gratitude stretches out endlessly before us and opportunities flourish everywhere for us to say thank you. We can say thank you for so much; we just have to see our fortuity. Our lives thrive with the countless possibilities and yet a single common theme lies at the core of each circumstance. Our appreciation of the gift, event, or whatever took place should be secondary to our appreciation for the person or people who showed us they cared. We give our appreciation to *people* not to objects. The object is an outcome of someone's feelings for us. The giver made this happen; the giver thought about us, and put those thoughts into action because he, she, or they care for us.

Families and friends are the foundation stones of our life. Do we grasp how important they are to us? What about those who are less visible? The person who delivers our mail (Yes, I know they bring bills too), our regular hairdresser, or perhaps the librarian who helped us to find that book we wanted. Do all these people know how much you appreciate what they do for you? Or should I ask do *you* know how much *you* appreciate what they do for you?

Thank You letters create a stronger personal connection with those who enrich your life. Let that person receive the focus of your gratitude and strengthen the bond between you.

The Letter versus the Note - Again!

We covered this topic in more detail earlier. The line is even less clear when expressing our gratitude and appreciation because both achieve the same effect. Now, without wishing to appear contradictory to what has already been stated, I should like you to accept a premise that the similarities between the thank you letter and note unite them into one entity. So for the rest of this chapter I shall still refer to the letter but can mean either. In the samples I have included, there is one sample note and three sample letters to give you a feel for both the similarities and differences.

Approach

Whether you choose a pre-printed card or use your own stationery is entirely up to you. The thoughts and sentiments which are expressed through your words are what counts. In the suggested outline below the term 'gift' represents not only the physical aspects such as a present but also the more intangible elements such as emotional support.

Seven pointers to follow for expressing your gratitude are:

- ❖ Always write it by hand.
- ❖ Be brief.
- ❖ Include the date and name of the person you want to thank.

Words for Letters

- ❖ Start and end with a Thank You.
- ❖ Mention the gift specifically and how it affects you.
- ❖ Keep the focus on your reader; it is not about you.
- ❖ Be hearty and warm.

Consider a simple handwritten note nicely placed in your friend's coat pocket. Short and sweet but says a lot.

Thank You Note Sample 1

27th December 2013

Dear Paula,
   Thank you for being the most considerate and understanding best friend in the entire universe!!!

Annie xxx

Thank You Letter Sample 1

The letter below is to-the-point, warm, and appreciative. The focus is clearly directed at the 'you' while the 'I' supports the sentiments and does not to steal the spotlight.

27th December 2012

Dear Martin,
   Thank you so much for the table lamp. It lights the hallway beautifully and brings such a welcoming feel into the house. I smile every time I walk past it. How very thoughtful of you to come up with such a wonderful gift!
   I wish you all the best for the New Year and hope to see you soon.
   Thanks again for the lamp – I love it!

Hugs,

Pam

Notice that Pam has not only explicitly acknowledged Martin's present but has also described its effect on the hallway and how it makes her smile. She is painting a picture and showing Martin how appreciative she is. Their friendship is evident through the way she has chosen to relate to him. Compare this with a simpler message perhaps sent electronically saying:

Martin – great present, awesome - thanks!

Which would you prefer to receive? Why is that? Reflect on the differences you see and jot them down in your notebook.

Thank you letters are such a wonderful medium to celebrate our friendships and create stronger bonds. Shall we try a different type of Thank You?

Thank You Letter Sample 2

8th August 2012

Dear Angela,

Your name gives your true self away. Thank you for being an angel to us these past few weeks. We simply could not have managed without your help. It cannot have been easy picking up our kids to and from school but they have so enjoyed travelling with you, and I get to hear all about the fun as soon as they burst through the door and dash upstairs.

Without your help, Doug would have had to take too much time off work which would not go down well at this time.

The doctor thinks I can get up for a few hours a day next week. Maybe even sit out on the porch for a little while.

Thank you for being there, not just lately but for the last forty years. No-one could have a better friend.

Love always,

Helen

The circumstances are more somber in the second sample letter. The appreciation is witnessed via Helen's children and her husband. Angela and Helen's friendship is firmly established and you would expect it to continue on well into the future. Just a few words can tell us so much about how we feel towards our friends. Think about this when you write your next thank you letter. Using the outline shown earlier in this chapter, ponder how you can weave your thoughts to include images to show your appreciation.

One final sample before moving on:

Thank You Letter Sample 3

4th May 2013

Hi Bob,

Thanks for dropping your drills off last Friday. Wow! They really do the job don't they? We must have saved days with what can only be described as pure magic! They make it so easy and the new shed looks brilliant!

Also, those shelves you recommended have created so much storage. The floor is clear so no more hopping and dodging to get to the workbench. This is no longer just a shed; this is now a castle, a fortress to take refuge in when the opportunity presents itself.

Thanks again – I'll drop your tools back round to yours during the week.

Cheers Buddy,

Al

Genuine and heartfelt gratitude forms the key element of a Thank You letter. Keep the focus on the person you are writing to, that person is the real reason for you to have something to be grateful for. Make sure to put them center stage.

Chapter 8

A Letter to Rekindle a Friendship

Be slow to fall into friendship; but when thou art in continue firm and constant.
~ Socrates ~

The clock crows. We wake. We shower. We dress. We eat. We leave. We drive. We work. We return. We eat. We chat. We tidy. We sleep. The day slides by, followed by another, and then another. The weeks chase the months into years. Where does all the time go?

Wake up and snap out of it!

The *real* alarm is trying to warn us that with each sharply scheduled moment of every overloaded day our friendships drift gently away into a swirl of fading recollections.

Regular texts and messages present us with the illusion of staying close but gradually their real meaning fragments and diminishes. The once considered thoughts surrender to superficial snippets. The gap between replies widens; the content becomes less contemplated and moves towards obligation rather than willful intention. Is this really how we want to treat our friends? Is this really how we want to treat ourselves?

Turning the Tide

Take a break from the demands of the day. Find that calm backwater for a few reflective moments. Allow your thoughts to find the friends with whom you have not recently spent time. Jot their names in your notebook along with a fond memory or exciting idea you would like to share with them. Make a commitment to get in touch with each one.

You are on your way to successfully starting to rekindle your friendship.

Write to your Friends

Your loved ones deserve your attention as you do theirs, whether they are close friends you have not seen lately or those living closer whom you have unintentionally failed to keep in touch. Do not let these relationships slip away any further. Act now. I suggest you handwrite your letter to them rather than use electronic communication. You are showing you have made more of an effort for them because you still value their friendship.

What to Say

Many people find difficulty in starting such a letter. Why does it feel so awkward? One explanation may be that we are growing too accustomed to short messages, or what appears to be the movement away from conversation towards announcement style communication. Applying an observation of economics, whereby if a resource becomes scarcer its worth rises, then empathy must hold an extremely high value. Check social networking comment streams to see if you agree. Instances of the 'me, myself and I' announcements are in abundance! Let us hope that this trend reverses. Are we simply out of practice with the more empathetic written communication?

Here is a little thought exercise to help you decide what to write. Imagine you meet your friend at a café with on-the-street tables. You sit enjoying the sun on your face and the scent of the flowers in the nearby box. Your friend arrives, drops shopping bags on one chair and plonks herself on the chair next to you. Envision what you would talk about. After the initial greeting, what topics might arise during the conversation? What memories do you think would be mentioned? Which bits of your news would you like to share?

The medium of the letter allows you to gather your thoughts and speak to your friend through your pen. You have the advantage of having time to think. Use a conversational voice in your letter.

Approach
Perhaps you might want to use the following guideline:

- ❖ Begin your letter in a very direct way. Aim to engage your friend's attention immediately rather than have them wondering why you have written.
- ❖ Portray a happy memory or two. Include a photograph if possible.
- ❖ Ask specific questions rather than general run-of-the-mill inquiries.
- ❖ Suggest planning to spend some time together.
- ❖ End with a reaffirmation of your friendship.
- ❖ Avoid vagueness.

Shall we see how these might work out?

Words for Letters

Friendship Rekindle Letter Sample 1

In this sample Liam writes to Sue. She is a friend he has not seen for a while.

> June 12, 2013
>
> Dear Sue,
>
> We never did finish our debate on whether roasted or mashed potatoes go better with roast beef. I have had plenty of time to stew over this and now believe I have the right ingredients to win the argument.
>
> Did you buy that car you were looking at so many times? The showroom staff probably started to think you worked there! Do you remember when we went camping just after you bought your old car? We had such a laugh; it's a wonder it made it up the hill with so much stuff packed in – you insisted on bringing so many pans and plates. Shame I forgot the camp-stove, eh? I have included a picture from the trip, see if you can remember the name of the couple who were in the tent next to us.
>
> I bumped into Anne and Dave; they asked how you were and I told them I had not seen you for a while, it's nearly six months! How did that happen?
>
> Sue, we all miss you. Do you think we could organize a get-together fairly soon?
>
> Smiles,
>
> Liam
>
> P.S. Be prepared with a good argument for the mashed potatoes. Better still we can all meet for a roast beef dinner!
> Enc: 1 photograph.

Notice how Liam ends the closing with a question which offers a way forwards. When Sue replies to this letter, the reunion will be a major topic. The debate on the potatoes is deliberately left unresolved and hence a proposed fun topic of conversation for their next meeting. It can be effective to introduce other people into the letter. Anne and Dave are mentioned and want to know how Sue is. Including a small detail like this indicates to Sue that she is still part of the group and her friends are still interested in her well-being.

Friendship Rekindle Letter Sample 2

This second sample is a letter from Tim to his friend Tony. They see each other more often than Sue or Liam in Sample 1 but haven't really spent any quality time together recently.

November 24, 2013

Dear Tony,

A new evening class called 'French for Beginners' has just been advertised in the library. I thought of you immediately and managed to get hold of the flyer. I have included it with this letter. It looks quite good and is at a reasonable time. All the details are on the flyer. Maybe a trip to Paris next April is worth considering?

Last year's trip to Chicago will take some beating! Pity we were a bit low on numbers this year to arrange anything. We just do not seem to have enough time to meet and chat anymore. Everyone seems busy dealing with all the snow this winter.

I propose that we reverse this always-busy-trend and start sorting some holiday time out. I will ask Sam, Jo, and Mike to see what ideas they have. If you would talk to Dave and Bernie then perhaps we can start things moving.

Let me know when would be a good time for us to meet up.

Take care Buddy,

Liam
Enc: 1

Once again we are establishing talking points of interest and suggesting a way forwards. If you are too vague the letter has no direction; better to focus on building an interest and suggesting an option.

Of course your friend may not like it or have a very different idea, but at least you are communicating and rekindling your friendship. You have re-opened the connection; a chance to re-establish your bond.

Chapter 9

A letter of Comfort

*No one is useless in this world,
who lightens the burden of it for anyone else.*
~ Charles Dickens ~

Darker moments appear in everyone's life causing upset and unpleasant feelings. Such sad occasions make us want to reach out and support our friends and help them cross the bridge to happier times. Our letter's purpose is not to try to fix a problem but to console, to offer reassurance, consideration, and love to our friends. We simply have to let them know we are there for them; *it's what friends do.*

In the context of this chapter the source of the unhappiness is not bereavement but events like an accident, unexpected job loss, or failing an important exam. The type of setbacks in life we do not plan for but nevertheless happen. We cover loss through bereavement in the chapter on the condolence letter.

When someone you care about experiences an unhappy event you may want to offer comfort but are unsure of how to approach writing a letter of this nature. What should you say? If you do not know what to say then you may feel useless and unable to help –

but you can. Follow your heart and with a little help, you will lighten the burden for those not as fortunate as you. So, how do you start?

First Steps

First and foremost find out what has actually happened and who was affected. Discreetly ask around to discover the cause of the distress. Avoid the temptation to jump straight in; you may only make matters worse. Neither should you delay until you are too late to offer any valuable support.

Different circumstances require different approaches. Once you have identified what has happened, assess the severity of the impact this has had on your friend so you can decide on the appropriate action. You need to discover as much as you can before you offer your support because the right support at the right time will be of the greatest value to those affected. Appropriate response is the key. You do not want to be over the top nor do you want to appear dismissive of a loved one's misfortune.

So, given such a potential of variation, how might you decide on how to approach this? If a minor incident has occurred then a telephone call to show your concern and offer your well wishes may be adequate. However, in more serious situations timing is important. You could write a short note either on writing paper or include your words into a 'Thinking of you' card. Perhaps something along the lines of:

Comfort Note Sample 1

August 15, 2012

Dear Paul and Joan,
We are sorry to hear that Joan has lost her job. We are thinking of you and would like to see you soon.

Lots of love.

Mark and Mary

In the above sample Mark and Mary have recognized their friends' misfortune and made them aware that they are supportive to them.

While you know *what* has happened, no one may yet know the *impact* this has and will have on the family; this may yet have to unfold over the days and weeks to come. Later may be the better time to write a letter (rather than note) of comfort and to offer help where it is now better understood to be needed.

Be yourself!

One advantage the letter has as a form of communication is that the recipient can choose when to read it and how often to read it. A telephone call or surprise visit may not be the ideal moment for you to approach your friends; they may still be too upset to be receptive to you. The letter creates the space for them to receive your support when they feel they are ready.

Writing the letter of comfort can seem like a difficult task. The most important aspect is the *message* you send - that you care and want to help. Your relationship to each of your friends is unique and so is every letter you write.

Guidelines

The suggestions below will help you to compose your letter. It may take more than one version so use scrap paper for the initial draft.

- ❖ Imagine yourself in their position. What would you like to read if you were facing these circumstances? This is one of the golden rules of letter writing.
- ❖ Say what you *feel*; this is an emotional time. BUT, do not trade bad experiences and relate how you have suffered in the past. No, No, and No! Remember this letter is <u>not about you</u> but to someone you care about who is probably emotionally vulnerable right now and still licking their wounds.

Words for Letters

- ❖ Do not offer to do anything that you cannot fulfill. No one wants to be offered broken promises.
- ❖ This letter only needs to say what it needs to say! Do not think you have to write pages and pages to tell your friends you recognize they are upset. Instead offer them comfort and to offer to help in any way *they* see fit.
- ❖ Invite them to reply or contact you.
- ❖ Use pastel colored stationery.
- ❖ Write a warm closing.

The sample letter below is a follow-up to the note sent earlier by Mark and Mary. If the note was sent within a day or two of Joan losing her job then this letter could follow a week later; either posted or discreetly hand delivered. How long you wait to send your letter is your choice and depends on what has occurred. Be mindful that your friends may have gone away for a break so a little undercover investigative work is advisable.

Comfort Letter Sample 1

August 20, 2012

Dear Paul and Joan,

We were so sorry to hear Joan's news and realize that this was a big shock to you both. It certainly was to us, and we feel for you at this time. Joan, you are such a talented lady and we are sure you will soon have success in finding a new position.

Both of us would dearly like to be of help to you but are unsure of what is best, and we do not want to appear invasive. Would you both come to supper on Tuesday night? We would very much like to see you. Just bring yourselves around seven.

Call us to let us know if you can come.

Lots of love,

Mark and Mary

Comfort Letter Sample 2.

Some clouds are darker than others. The second letter sample is one of the hardest to write, but do not let that put you off. Your friends will appreciate your concern and support. Do not abandon your friends in times of need, no matter how awkward it may feel to put pen to paper.

March 15, 2010

Dear Tom,

We heard about Liz's bad news and send you our warmest wishes. We hope her treatment is going well and that she will make a successful recovery.

This must have come as a shock to both of you but at least Liz is receiving the care she needs to help her get better. We will go and visit her as soon as it is possible to do so and she feels well enough to see us.

How are you feeling? We would like to come and visit you soon but we understand you have a lot to do right now. If you would let us know when would be best, we can sort out our travel arrangements and be with you in just a few hours.

Please give Liz our love and let her know we are thinking of her. She is such a wonderful lady and special friend.

Look after yourself and we look forwards to seeing you soon.

Hugs,

Larry and Grace

One other point you may wish to consider is that other people may have been affected by what has happened. Would you like to reach out to them too? Follow the same actions: you know what has happened; asses the distress this has caused to others; and determine what comfort you can offer.

Chapter 10

A Letter of Encouragement

What would life be like if we had no courage to attempt anything?
~ Vincent Van Gogh ~

Are you good at spotting 3D problems? You know the kind of problems I am talking about; those made up of Drifting, Deferring, and Doubting. A three pronged attack sucking your energy and draining you. Perhaps you see your friends struggling to reach their goals. Good News! You can replace the 3-Ds with 3-Es: Engaging, Empathizing, and Encouraging.

We sometimes underestimate how we can help others achieve their dreams. A little reassurance at the right time refreshes their efforts to meet their goals. Think of your own achievements. Did you experience those murky moments of stalling and meandering along the way? We have those days when we inch our way forward through the day and yet fall further behind each time we move; how can that be? We ache for the night and the chance to escape our frustration. We wish, from the sanctuary of our pillow, for daybreak to recharge us with new purpose and determination. But that is not always the case, is it? No, our lack of sleep enfeebles our mind, the doubts settle in right through us like a paralyzing frost.

How has it come to this? A single event could have stopped us in our tracks or perhaps we have gradually drifted off track.

.

The 3D View

Do you know someone who could benefit from a helping hand? Several influences may cause their stagnation but for now we will concentrate on the 3-Ds.

Drifting might appear if your friends have to make a decision or do something but do not know what to do or which course of action to follow. They begin to focus on matters elsewhere.

Deferring their decision or other outstanding activities may be the underlying issue. Have they stepped outside of their comfort zone? As their friend, you will see their issues from a different viewpoint. You are in a position to help.

Doubting their own ability to continue or to reach their goal may prove disastrous and have a further ripple effect in other aspects of their lives.

If you know someone who is languishing in the doldrums, I ask you to write a letter of encouragement to them. It is, after all, one of the reasons you bought this book. Why a letter? Why not just send a text or social media message or even call them? Well, you can do that too. Spoken words are excellent but they only happen in a single instance. Important undertones may be missed or misunderstood. Your letter enjoys the advantage of delivering your considered encouragement without your friend interrupting or pouring despair onto your supportive comments. Additionally, re-reading your letter may spark an inspiration to kick start their project with renewed vigor. Your written words carry an ongoing healing comfort through the belief you have in your friend.

Bring out the shoebox immediately and get to it! No waiting around. Now is the time to write and offer your encouragement. We both know you can do it!

Words for Letters

EEEs it forwards

Engaging with your friends helps you to better understand their predicament. What is the root cause of the issue? What can you do to find out more about their situation? Do a little research.

Empathizing moves you closer to the problem and how your friend is affected. Be mindful that what you may not see as an obstacle others may see as a huge hurdle. In life we all bring something different to the party.

Encouraging your friend to move forward is your gift to them. No point in just milling around and shaking your head. Do not dig the hole any deeper. You are involved now so you must provide encouragement to progress to the next step and ultimately to a successful conclusion.

Guidelines

The structure of your letter can be based upon the following:

- ❖ Identify the issue.
- ❖ Recognize the impact this may have.
- ❖ Remind your friends they have a goal.
- ❖ Encourage your friend to move forward, possibly offer some suggestions for further discussion.
- ❖ Suggest, if feasible, a face to face discussion.

As always, remember this letter is *not about you* but your friends. Your support is aimed towards them.

Encouragement Letter Sample 1

The scenario: Malcolm wants to improve his position at the company he works for. He has applied to the company's training department to fund an external course which will improve his skills and understanding, thus giving him a better chance to move into a team leader role. The company has considered his application but has rejected it. Malcolm still wants to improve his position but feels defeated as a result of the company turning down his funding request.

Marie, one of his friends, writes the following letter to him.

August 15, 2013

Dear Mal,

Susan told me about the rejection of your application for funding. I was sorry to hear that. Dave and Jo asked me to pass on their regards to you – I saw them yesterday.

We all feel disappointed too, because we have known you long enough to recognize that you put one hundred percent into everything you do. This is a setback, but not the end of it. You must continue to keep sight of the team leader role. This is your goal. There will be another route to this. Can you think of any destination that has only one route to it? No? Well, neither can anyone else.

Dave, Jo and I have decided to interfere. It's our right to do so as your friends. Time for you to get back on track! No excuses! I have enclosed two brochures on courses similar to the one you mentioned. Both are run by colleges here in town, in the evenings and on a part-time basis. They are much more affordable and carry the same level of recognition as your original intended course. Yes, it does mean two evenings per week commitment from you but we know you will easily do that. And besides, you can join us at the coffee bar on Main Street afterwards on one of the nights. Take a look at the brochure and see what you think.

Speaking of coffee, Jo is on one of her baking missions. We are congregating at her house on Saturday for coffee and to unashamedly devour her cakes. I expect you to bring your best smile with you. You and I can have a little chat about the next steps you are going to take.

Your bossiest friend ever,

Marie

Isn't Marie a great friend to have? Maybe a little bossy, but a true friend – there are too few of them in the world. The Maries of this world keep it turning so the sun can rise every day for all of us.

Encouragement Letter Sample 2

Make the letters fun to write and read when the opportunity arises. Keeping the subject lively automatically adds energy and a positive approach. In such cases never be frightened to exaggerate or write outlandish comments. Your friend will grasp your sentiments.

May 3, 2013

Dear Frank,

Word has it you are having second thoughts about taking up hot air ballooning. These negative thoughts are to be banished henceforth!

How can this be so? We look to you for inspiration. You are our guiding light. Once you have passed the exams with flying colors you will be able to take us on exciting expeditions.

You will lead us on adventures as we cross the skies to new lands full of mystery and daring feats - yes, I understand 15 miles round trip is not exactly pioneering, but let us dream!

This is not a time for doubts as the age of discovery lies at your feet. Chin up old bean and best foot forward.

You are 'Fearless Frank' the soon-to-be intrepid balloonist extraordinaire and adventurous aviator.

Your swashbucklers of the skies,

Lady Iterringham and Lord Polo

Chapter 11

A Letter of Condolence

Unable are the loved to die. For love is immortality.
~ Emily Dickinson ~

We choose the path on which to travel through life. Each day our feet step, stroll, trudge, amble, stumble, traipse, stagger, saunter, prance, strut, stride, slog or march as we make our headway. Each crossroad defines a new stage and each corner masks what lies waiting beyond. Others join our path and we travel together until each and every one of us reaches the point of rest; our journey's end.

The bereaved's world changes forever in a single instance of passing; heartbreak and despair settles onto their hearts. Before they continue they must first pick up the scattered shards lying on their path. As friends, we must offer our sympathy, be sensitive, and help in any way we can.

Please remember the focal point is not about you. You may be affected too, but your letter of condolence shows the bereaved that you see *they* are grieving, share *their* sadness, recognize *their* loss, and offer support to *them*.

Words for Letters

Take your Time

This is a single occasion letter; it relates to a unique circumstance that has befallen others. Your connection, in these sad circumstances, may lead to further communications, and given time, develop into a deeper connection filled with news and topics that friends like to share with each other.

The gravity of a loved one's passing demands much more consideration than other types of letters because of the emotional vulnerability of all those affected. You may be upset too and find it painful to say what you want. This is understandable, so take your time.

Please do not expect to write this letter at the first attempt. It may take several rewrites. Use your notebook to jot down phrases and expressions you might want to say. I suggest the notebook rather than scrap paper because these letters are a challenge and you may want to keep your thoughts in one place and possibly reflect on them should you need to offer your condolences to others in the future.

Considerations

Sit down with your notebook and contemplate on the following:

- ❖ How long is it since the deceased passed? If within a week the shock may still be overwhelming. The bereaved are busy making funeral arrangements and numerous notifications so perhaps a sympathy note rather than a letter is wiser at this stage. The note can be in addition to any calls or face-to-face conversations
- ❖ You may choose to buy and send a sympathy card; this is common practice because some of those cards do convey their message well. However, you are conveying your personal message through a third party's words; is this what you want? Does the verse inside say exactly what you want it to? How personal is it? People often

choose a card because they think it says what they *ought* to say. Before you decide to buy a card, compose a few words which you would say face-to-face if your bereaved friend was sitting in front of you. Your words would express your true feelings. When choosing your card, read the verse and ask yourself if it expresses the same feelings as your words. Are you satisfied to swap your words for a scripted verse? What do you think is the likelihood of the bereaved receiving the same card from different people as opposed to two handwritten notes saying the exact same words? If you find a card you are happy with, you could include your own words or a note to make your message even more personal.

- To whom are you writing? You may have known the deceased but not the bereaved. Imagine your friend has moved far away and subsequently married someone they met in their new location. If your friend died, you may want to write a letter of condolence to your friend's surviving partner even though you have never met each other. In this instance, place the emphasis on your deceased friend and shared experiences which enriched your life. Remember to keep the focus on your friend not you. If however, it was your friend's spouse who had died and whom you had never met, then the emphasis has to be on supporting your friend.

- Do you need to write to more than one person? This could arise if, for example, a father of a family has died and there are teenage children in the family. You may decide to write to the children too.

- When composing your letter, reflect on how the bereaved are likely to feel when they read it – immediately, days, weeks, months or years later. Your letter may be included in a scrapbook or part of a memoir or as a testimony the deceased. How might it fit into those scenarios? Be mindful that other mourners too will probably read your note or letter.

Words for Letters

- ❖ When a death occurs we must respect the wishes of the bereaved on how the sad news will be announced. Please do not place messages immediately on social media or other communication media because this is not only disrespectful but you may be seen as trying to put yourself center stage.
- ❖ When choosing your words, be careful about using religious references; not everyone has the same beliefs. Do a little tactful research to determine if the bereaved would appreciate such a reference.
- ❖ If you lack confidence in your letter writing skills, your spelling or your grammar, do not worry. Never let any such fears or inhibitions hold you back. Your sentiments will touch their heart. This is a very important letter of support and love not an appraisal of writing skills.
- ❖ Be appropriate and have a sense of perspective and propriety. How close were you to the deceased or bereaved? Be honest. Neither exaggerate nor understate your relationship. You can say so much in just a few words. It is not just the words that count but who said them which makes them special. You must assess the degree of formality, the closer you are, the more personal the letter.
- ❖ Always write something. Your words are support; your silence conveys cold anonymity. If you are unsure of what to write just follow your heart. The words will come. No communication at all may be interpreted as ignoring or even forsaking those in their moments of need.

Guidelines for the Condolence Note

Circumstances are always unique because of how the deceased may have died and the effect this may have on others. As mentioned earlier, the note presents your condolences in the immediate aftermath of a death. The suggested guidelines below are there to help you; the words and sentiments will ultimately be yours. Your relationship with the deceased and those affected is as individual as you are and so should your sentiments be.

- ❖ Start with a warm and personal greeting.
- ❖ Acknowledge the loss of the deceased.
- ❖ Briefly mention a special characteristic of the person.
- ❖ Offer a specific way to help, not a generic one.
- ❖ Finish with a personal and warm closing.
- ❖ Keep the note brief.

Below are sample notes followed by two sample letters.

Note of Condolence Sample 1

In this note sample Linda is immediately acknowledging her friend's loss, showing an appreciation of the family's feelings and offering to do something practical. In this case she offers extra coffee, tea, and milk because there may be visitors to the grieving family's house. It is simple, practical and thoughtful.

November 25, 2012

My dearest Alex,

I am sorry to hear about the death of your father, Harry. We will all miss his hearty laugh. I understand you are all saddened and shocked at this time.

Would it help if I dropped off extra coffee, tea, and milk for you?

With all my love,

Linda

Words for Letters

Note of Condolence Sample 2

In the second sample the writer did not know the deceased and therefore focuses on the bereaved. Once again the offer is very simple and requires a straightforward answer.

September 23, 2013

Dear Pete,

I was never lucky enough to meet Adele; she certainly captured your heart and made you so happy. She changed your life as only someone special can. I am very sorry for your loss. Would you like me to tell everyone you worked with at our office?

Your friend always,

Mark

Note of Condolence Sample Letter 3

This next sample is from Dave who speaks straight from his heart. The honesty and love pours out all over the page and says so much in just a few simple words.

January 5, 2014

Dear Sue,

You know I am not good at writing, but I loved your grandma a lot. She smiled a lot and her pot pies were the best. I will miss her loads.

Dave

The Condolence Letter

Once the immediate shock has waned and the grieving process starts, your support is still needed. Having sent your note earlier you can write a condolence letter to add memories of the deceased, the effect they had, and become more reflective in your tone.

Perhaps you did not hear about the deceased's passing until weeks or months afterwards. No matter, you can still write to send your condolences. Warmhearted expressions of sympathy and support are always welcomed.

Here are the guidelines for the letter; they expand on what we said earlier in the note because the letter plays a different role.

- Start with a warm and personal greeting.
- Acknowledge the loss of the deceased.
- Express your sympathy.
- Cite characteristics of the deceased you liked.
- Add a special memory.
- Include words of encouragement.
- Offer a specific way to help.
- Close in a warm way.

As you can see, this is similar to the note structure but the emphasis has changed. We are moving towards supporting our friends over the longer term as the realization of loss through the 'little things in life' plays a part in the grieving.

Let us look at a sample.

Words for Letters

Letter of Condolence Sample 1

In this sample Arthur and Cathy write to Pauline whose brother passed recently. Read the sample and jot down your thoughts about each paragraph. What picture of the relationships does this letter show you? What might you like to add or change?

14th January 2013

Dear Pauline

Thank you for inviting us to your brother's funeral. We did not think it was possible for the Chapel of Rest to hold so many people.

Ken was so popular in our village; a great loss to those whose lives he touched. Everyone will remember him for his enthusiasm and willingness to bring the village closer together.

Yesterday Pat, Liz, and Norma were helpless with laughter as we recalled Ken's famous beard shaving incident at the summer fair two years ago. Who would have thought it possible to trap their beard in a cake carrier? It defies belief! Although let's not forget the money it raised for the dog rescue services. Ken was one of those people you meet in life who makes a difference to those around him.

You two were always so close; you must miss him so much. Move forwards with Ken still in your heart. We are all fortunate to have known such a good man and we are all grateful to be able to carry memories of him with us wherever we go and in whatever we do.

You said you were going to finish the shed he was working on out in his yard next week. Would it be okay if we helped you with that?

Arthur thought you might like to join us on Friday for dinner; if you are free let us know what time would be best for you.

See you soon,
Arthur and Cathy

Words for Letters

Letter of Condolence Sample 2

This next sample is similar but different. The structure is similar but we are dealing with a different type of loss. Compare the two letters and jot down just a couple of points where you think they are different. Consider how these two sample letters differ from the three sample notes given earlier in this chapter.

June 25, 2013

Dear Geoff,

How many people can say they lived life to its fullest? Well, Martha came as close as anyone could. What a character she was! Her death is still a huge shock to everyone and we are saddened by your loss. Martha is in our hearts and her life shows us how important every minute is. We love her dearly.

We were looking through the many photographs we have of you both; so many happy memories to cherish. After a somewhat 'competitive' discussion we agreed that the most outstanding moment we were lucky to be part of was our holiday with you in 1998. Remember we booked those riding lessons and on the first day before we had even left the stables Martha had lost her pony!!!!! The instructor just stood there aghast! Only Martha would go on the offensive and blame the pony for deserting her.

Her eccentricities and wild behavior has had us in tears so often and today those tears still flow because, like you, we all miss her.

Now, Geoff you must continue both her and your good work in the garden. We always look forward to sharing your homegrown vegetables and herbs.

When we spoke last week you mentioned you would like to donate Martha's clothes to the charity shop. Before you do that I would like to have one of her beautiful scarves; you know, just something to keep close to me. Would you like us to come and help you sort through everything?

Although Martha has left, we still look forwards to spending so many more happy times with you, Geoff.

All our love,
Molly and Jan

Chapter 12

A Letter of Recommendation

No bird soars too high, if he soars with his own wings.
~ William Blake ~

If you are familiar with expressions relating to banana skins, double-edged swords or Achilles heel, you are in the right territory for this chapter. Writing a letter of recommendation is a balancing act. Even with the purest intentions in mind, it is possible to present the reference in the wrong light and compromise both your own and another's integrity.

We all enjoy helping others advance to their goals but we do have a duty to all those involved. On the one hand we do not want to overstate character and capabilities in our recommendation but on the other hand we should not undermine qualities. These inaccuracies turn our recommendation into misrepresentation whether intentional or not. Thus we must strive to ensure a fair and true portrayal of what we have been asked to provide and be comfortable that we can deliver that information with due diligence and honesty.

Unsettled

Writing a letter of recommendation or providing a reference should bolster your friend or colleague's chances of achievement. But what do you write? What does it entail? Are you sufficiently qualified to write such a letter? Perhaps this is the first time you have been asked to do this and you feel intimidated by the prospect of such a responsibility. You do not want to let anyone down and yet feel like you have been cut adrift on a raft and are uncertain of what to do next, all of which is perfectly natural.

Preparation is the key. Have you noticed how this is prevalent in letter writing? Of course it is. We are taking the time and effort (notice I did not say 'time and trouble' because this is a pleasurable task) to help someone accomplish another step up their ladder. If a successful outcome ensues, you can be assured that all went according to plan.

Warning

Suppose you have been asked to write a recommendation for someone you do not know that well. You may feel uncomfortable about doing it purely for that reason or you may think that you are being inappropriately used. Do not accept their request to provide the reference. Refuse politely and explain you are not in a position to help them on this occasion.

Guidelines

The challenge is writing to someone you may have never met and to recommend someone whom the person you are writing to may have only met very briefly. On the face of it, that does look like a recipe for disaster but you can do it. Look at the guidelines below and determine your plan of action.

- ❖ Ensure you have the details of whom you are writing to. No bonus points are awarded for sending it to the wrong person or address. The outcome will be that everyone looks stupid! In the case where the recipient's name is

- unavailable, addressing your letter 'To whom it may concern' or 'Dear Sir or Madam' is acceptable.
- ❖ Be clear about the what, where, and why you are recommending your friend or colleague.
- ❖ Cite specifics that are relevant. Ask which points need to be covered and in what priority. Suppose your friend is applying for the role of chef, there is no point in praising her skills as a musician! Only include what is needed.
- ❖ State the capacity in which you know the person and how long you have known them.
- ❖ Be realistic. Do not make any exaggerations; the truth will come out eventually and you may regret damage befalling your credibility.
- ❖ Add any personal comments towards the end and complete your letter by offering further information if required.
- ❖ Spelling and grammar are more important here as your credibility is at stake.
- ❖ You might consider using a typed letter on letterhead stationery if the context is business, academic or professional.

Check and double check the points above. You must fully understand what you have been asked to do and feel confident that you have prevented any potential slipping on banana skins.

Letter of Recommendation Sample 1

Make sure you include the date to protect the letter from being photocopied and subsequently used without your knowledge or permission. This is especially true when you are using 'To whom it may concern' in the salutation.

Address
February 10, 2013

To whom it may concern,

I would like to recommend Alan Smith for the Marketing Masters program at your university. I have known Alan for three years; he is a talented young man who works hard, has a positive attitude, and enjoys his studies. Alan has many fine attributes; my favorite is his dedication and determination to develop a concept or technique through to a meaningful fruition.

I had the privilege of being his tutor throughout his Bachelor's program interacting with him on a weekly basis. He worked hard over the three years and made outstanding progress. In addition, he has become an excellent presenter and skilled communicator.

Alan enjoyed receiving recognition from outside of the faculty too.

- *He came first in the Young People's Business Awards for our State.*
- *He has had marketing articles published in two industry related magazines.*
- *He successfully completed an internship with a prominent online shopping company.*

As a person, Alan is very dependable, well prepared, and committed to give you his best and honest efforts. His enthusiasm is infectious and he is well liked by his fellow students.

If you would like any further information please do not hesitate to contact me.

Yours sincerely,

Professor D. Tambling
(Include additional contact information if required.)

Chapter 13

A Letter of Vengeance

*Revenge is not always sweet,
once it is consummated we feel inferior to our victim.*
~ Emil Cioran ~

One rule only:
Never threaten anyone for any reason in a letter.
It's simply not done!

Chapter 14

A letter of Apology

Never ruin an apology with an excuse.
~ Benjamin Franklin ~

Is it worth crying over? When we make a mess we ought to take responsibility and clean it up. Do not ignore it and hope it will blow over, that choice may just make matters worse. An apology is the first step to healing and rebuilding. A step forward moves us to a brighter future and a mending of the past.

No Buts

Under no circumstances must the word 'but' appear after an apology; if we do include it then we have demeaned the apology and it is worthless. An apology is an apology; it is not an excuse.

On occasion we all mess up; that's life. When we take responsibility to put things right, we choose the right course of action. Our first step is to make an apology to those whom we have hurt. Once we sit down to write an apology, a few harsh truths must be faced. We do not go looking for any sympathy because we do not deserve it. We swallow our pride; hold our hands up and try to get everything back on track for everyone, not just ourselves.

Before you consider what we might or might not write in the letter, contemplate your desired outcome from making this apology. Is it redemption or forgiveness you are seeking? Unfortunately, that is all about you, so skip to the next chapter. However, if you want to let whomever you have hurt know that you are genuinely sorry and look to move forward together building a more positive relationship, then carry on reading this chapter.

So, how do you do this?

The Golden rule of letter writing must be evident throughout the letter – the focus is not on you but on the person you are writing to. You might consider using to the 3-3-3 approach to try and recover the situation: 3 thoughts, 3 considerations, and 3 paragraphs.

You will need the support of your shoebox to begin your preparations. Your scrap paper and notebook are your initial building blocks. Plan on more than one sitting. A relationship or friendship worth saving deserves to be respected and taken seriously.

Effort and directed thinking is essential to start the reparation work. You might not like some of the aspects that surface but shape your thoughts to stop them from preventing this healing and rebuilding.

Three Thoughts

Before you start, consider:

- ❖ What is it you want to achieve from writing this letter?
- ❖ What exactly are you apologizing for and why?
- ❖ What do you want to happen next?

Scribble your thoughts on your scrap paper.

Why are you making an apology? Is it because of something you did, or did not do? Who did this affect? What is your relationship with those who are upset and how has this changed?

Three Considerations
Your letter will only say what it needs to say and no more.

- ❖ Always make your apology unconditionally.
- ❖ Do not rush and expect too much.
- ❖ Be very careful if your actions resulted in some form of loss to others; you may receive a letter from an attorney in reply. If in doubt consult an attorney.

I should like to say that common sense would prevail, but as you and I both know, that is not always the case. Keep a sense of perspective in your letter by avoiding excessive explanations.

Three Paragraphs
Your letter will be tactful but direct. Do not skirt around any matters that need to be addressed or try to cloud the issue. If your intention is to rebuild the relationship then let the person know that.

- ❖ Be polite and show warmth. Remember, at this point you are walking on eggshells.
- ❖ Admit you are in the wrong and offer your apology unconditionally – no buts, no deflecting, no watering down.
- ❖ Offer a way forward.

Letter of Apology Sample 1
Letters of apology are strong statements of your character. In the long run friends respect each other for having the courage to stand up and apologize. As we walk down life's paths the bumpy bits make us appreciate the smoother parts.

October 10, 2013

Dear Martha,

    You were kind to invite us to your anniversary dinner last Thursday and I thank you sincerely for that.

    I am ashamed at allowing myself to argue publicly with Joe. I embarrassed you in front of your friends and family and am deeply sorry to have hurt you. It was very foolish of me, and I have learned a valuable lesson from this. I offer you my unreserved apologies and ask for your forgiveness.

    We have been friends for such a long time, and I do not want to lose you as one of my closest friends. I want to offer you an olive branch. Would you please meet me for coffee next week?

Your friend,

Peter

Chapter 15

The Annual Holiday Letter

*There is something curiously boring
about someone else's happiness.*
~ Aldous Huxley ~

December offers us the ideal opportunity to overindulge our families and friends with news of our amazing feats. We risk overfeeding them with words of self-declared glory disguised as a holiday letter. We go on and on and on and on. Their festive spirits drain with the strain of reading our crowing. We bore them. The holiday letter, when written this way presents hibernation as an attractive alternative.

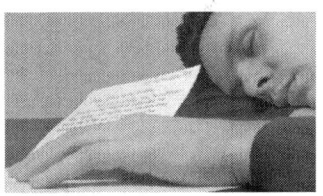

Suppose our family and friends simply do not care about our detailed achievements? We annoy them, worse still; their green-eyed monster could stir within. Was this our intention? I doubt it, but we have heard about roads paved with good intentions.

Onerous
Do you and those around you find writing the Holiday Letter a chore or a pleasure?

Do you find reading them burdensome? There must be a way to compose holiday letters to create interest and not encourage impromptu siestas?

The approach below aims to help you write your holiday letter with the minimum amount of effort and fuss. If previously you found this a chore you may now find it a pleasure but the real proof of success lies with your reader's reaction.

Do they find reading your holiday letter a chore or a pleasure?

Approach

Begin by looking at why we write a holiday letter. Look at these three suggestions and see if you agree or disagree or if you have other aims.

- ❖ To keep in touch once a year.
- ❖ To fill your letter with news not boasts.
- ❖ To create a record for the family by keeping a copy in a scrapbook.

So far so good, but wait a minute, two vital questions spring to mind:

- ❖ To whom do you write?
- ❖ Do you write the same letter to everyone?

The first question will take some thought and the answer might change as you go along. What starts as a simple straightforward task can soon blossom into a heavy millstone if you lose control. Preparatory work and a plan will help to keep you on track and save you both time and frustration.

Are you ready to start the plan? First of all, make an up-to-date list of recipients. If you have one from last year, start with that. Make a copy of last year's list. Now sort the people into groups. Work along the following lines.

Words for Letters

- ❖ Mark those friends you keep in touch with regularly – face-to-face, telephone, social media etc. They know your news and have already dismissed it from their minds. Do not put them through that experience a second time. Perhaps replace their letter with just a festive card and a simple handwritten message included on the card. However, if they request 'the letter' send them one.
- ❖ Remove the following from your list.
  - ➢ Anyone who has died.
  - ➢ Anyone who stopped sending you cards this year; they have probably moved – or no longer wish to be associated with you. These things happen. Look on the positive side; you save the cost of a stamp.
  - ➢ Anyone you no longer wish to be on the list. It's your list after all.
  - ➢ Check that everyone's address details are current. The address book in your shoebox is useful. Do not waste time duplicating the address by writing it on your list. Too many things can go wrong when copying address details so let the address book be the main oracle. Avoid having the same information in more than one place.
  - ➢ Remove anyone from the list whose address you are unsure of.
- ❖ Add new friends and acquaintances.
- ❖ Categorize the remaining people on your list.
  - ➢ Decide on which people fall into the *outer circle* – they will receive a generic printed letter but within a handwritten envelope.
  - ➢ Choose your *inner circle*. These are your close family and friends who live far away or those you have not seen for a while. They deserve a little more attention. You will handwrite this group's letter. Should you feel you do not want to make the extra

effort for them, they should be moved to the outer circle. Try to keep this list to a minimal number.
- ❖ Never send a printed letter in an envelope with a printed label unless your intention is to have yourself removed from their list for the following year! They will not appreciate your effort because you have not made any!

You have your two groups. Open your well stocked shoebox and check its contents. You are looking for specific items.

- ❖ Festive related stationery.
- ❖ Matching ink.
- ❖ A word processor font for the outer circle. Okay, I accept you will not find the word processor font in the shoebox!
- ❖ A festive themed stamp.

These next five points apply to both groups:

- ❖ Keep the letter as brief as possible.
- ❖ Do not flood the letter with achievements. A gushing fountain of kudos soon washes away your reader's interest. They are happy to learn how you are; not read your attainment list.
- ❖ Summarize the year for each person mentioned in a couple of sentences. If you have children and they ask to write their own letter then let them do so. Do not tell your children what to write. They will write about what is important to them not you! Respect that.
- ❖ Use words to create imagery rather than dull facts.
- ❖ Look back on previous letters you may have sent or received. Examine how they start. What do they actually say? Look at what catches your interest and think about why. Scribble a few thoughts on how you can make your letter attractive.

Writing to the Outer Circle

Practicality suggests that some form of printed letter suits this group. Keep the letter warm and simple with a touch of festive spirit. These are your friends, and you want them to know that.

Holiday Letter Sample 1

Let us start with a partial sample of what **not** to write in a holiday letter. The comments included in brackets are not part of the letter but possibly the reader's thoughts.

> *December 12, 2010*
>
> *Our dearest friends,* [Are we? We do have names. Sincerity?]
>   *It is that time of year again.* [yawning already] *What a great year we have had!!!! Jenny has been promoted twice at work and is now a K7* [when she reaches K9 will she be in the dog-house?] *She is in charge of two teams.* [Interest is waning] *How well she has done!* [We get the point] *We are so proud of her.* [Really? Move on!] *It is only four years since she left school, and to think she was a classmate of your son Peter. Has he got a job yet?* [Grrr!]
> *....*

You can see where this letter is heading – straight to the bin probably. Jenny's parents are obviously very pleased and proud of their daughter but bragging has no place in a holiday letter.

Words for Letters

Holiday Letter Sample 2

Look at the second sample below. How does this differ from the previous one? What images or feelings does this letter invoke for you?

December 12, 2009

Dear family and friends,

The annual return of Mary's holiday recipe book to pole position on the kitchen counter sets my taste buds racing. Smells of freshly baked cakes waft through the house. I love this time of year!

In preparation to writing this letter we looked through our photograph albums at this year's pictures. We were reminded of how much we have enjoyed being with you all at various times and we thank you for so many happy memories.

Mary is the same as ever, she has recently taken up swimming again and enjoys it immensely. David has moved into an apartment much nearer to his work and enjoys more free time because of the shorter commute. Paula continues to clutter the house with her sports gear but now has a car and is much freer to travel to the venues. As for me, well, the operation on my knee went well and I am back out cycling a couple of times per week.

Distance prevents us from sharing Mary's magical chocolate cake with many of you this year, but we do offer our warmest wishes to you all.

Enjoy the holidays,

Michael, Mary, David, & Paula

You might choose to use a special font on your computer to write the letter. As soon as you are happy with it, load your selected stationery into your printer and print the letters. Perhaps ask someone to help you with the envelopes; maybe read out the addresses to you. Handwrite the envelopes, pop the festive stamps on, and post them. All done, reward your efforts by patting yourself on the back, putting your feet up, and enjoying your best-loved small treat.

Writing to the Inner Circle

These people are closer to you and want to hear your news; they may already know most of it but will value the effort you have made for them. Write to each of these by hand; the aim is to keep the letter brief but with a little more personal touch.

Writing each letter by hand may seem daunting at this point. What are you going to say to each person or family? You may fear that it will take forever; that the holiday period will have come and gone by the time you have finished writing them all. That may be true if we have to compose each letter individually. We must adopt a tactical approach – or slightly cheat as some might say – to reduce the amount of effort.

The composition is where all the time is taken, not the actual writing by hand. The goal is to reduce the composition time so why not use the same wording you used in the letter to the outer circle but add a personal paragraph? Yes, it does work!

Important Final Preparations

How do you do it? Well, set aside three to four hours, a bar of chocolate (or whatever you like) for emergencies, and commandeer someone – or several people - to bring you tea or coffee every hour or to perform other supportive minor tasks. You are the general and this is a coordinated effort! You are in charge, probably because nobody else wants to write the letter. Therefore, they have a duty to support and serve you!

Look at the third sample. I have included suggestions of how this can be adapted to a more personal level in brackets. These are the parts to change to suit each addressee.

Holiday Letter Sample 3

December 12, 2009

Dear [Paul and Andrea]

The annual return of Mary's holiday recipe book to pole position on the kitchen counter sets my taste buds racing. Smells of freshly baked cakes waft through the house. I love this time of year.

In preparation to writing this letter we looked through our photograph albums at this year's pictures. We were reminded of how much we have enjoyed being with you. [Do you remember our trip to the park and Paul and I got stuck in the snow by the fountain? Looking back, wasn't that hilarious? The embarrassment of being 'rescued' by those two policemen. We laughed so much about this.]

Mary is the same as ever, she has recently taken up swimming again and enjoys it immensely. David has moved into an apartment much nearer to his work and enjoys more free time because of the shorter commute. Paula continues to clutter the house with her sports gear but now has a car and is much freer to travel to the venues. As for me, the operation on my knee went well and I am back out cycling a couple of times per week.

Distance prevents us from sharing Mary's magical chocolate cake with many of you this year but we do offer our warmest wishes to you all.[We both hope that next year will soon bring you to our doorstep once more.]

[Our love always,]

Michael, Mary, David, & Paula

From time to time unhappy events overshadow the year. Do not try to hide them nor dwell on them. People will understand that in sad circumstances you cannot be bubbling over with happiness nor should you pretend to.

The sample below is based on the two previous samples but is written under very different circumstances.

Your turn to do work again; grab your pencil and rapidly filling notebook. Compare this next sample with the last two and jot down how and why this letter makes you feel differently. How might you handle this?

Holiday Letter Sample 4

December 12, 2009

Dear family and friends,

Our first holiday without Mary has arrived. She is dearly missed by all of us, both near and far. Her spirit lives on in our hearts and to that end we are going to try our best to recreate the magical chocolate cake in her honor.

David has moved into an apartment much nearer to his work and enjoys more free time because of the shorter commute. Paula continues to clutter the house with her sports gear but now has a car and is much freer to travel to the venues. As for me, the operation on my knee went well and I am back out cycling a couple of times per week.

Distance prevents us from sharing our table with many of you this year but we do offer our warmest wishes to you all and hope our paths cross next year.

Yours as ever,

Michael, David, & Paula

Chapter 16

A Love Letter

The best gifts are tied with heartstrings.
~ Unknown ~

We wish to tell someone we love them. But who are we telling and why? Are we in a relationship with him or her? That is the usual assumption but what about writing to grandparents who live far away and we want to tell them how much we love them. Is that not a form of love letter too? What about our children? We tell them we love them. Consider someone who has been a close friend over the years, someone you can confide in, trust in, and someone who always has your best interest at heart – is such a friend not worthy of a love letter?

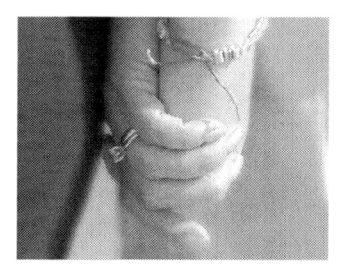

Why?

I propose – and expect you to second – that we can write a love letter to anyone we are close to. Why would we do this? Our friends and family are our greatest comfort throughout our life. Let us look at some of the reasons why we write love letters:

Words for Letters

- To tell our partner that he or she are a special to us and that we love them
- To tell someone who is away for an extended period that we miss him or her
- To tell a close friend you appreciate something very special he or she has done for us or our family.
- To simply say 'I love you'
- To tell a friend he or she is not alone

Many other reasons exist and I am sure you can think of people or circumstances in which to write a love letter.

Can you not just tell the person face to face? Yes, but you may not always have the opportunity to use the best words in a conversation. Sitting down to write a letter in solitude encourages your thoughts to wander along creative paths and find more affectionate expressions for your feelings, and without interruption. Your letter carefully woven from the threads of your heart creates a warm and personal articulation of your feelings with a sense of permanency. Imagine grandchildren with tears of joy as they read old letters showing how much Grandpa and Grandma have always dearly loved each other.

Suggested Guidelines

Three thoughts to bear in mind while composing your letter will help you to make it special.

- This is a very personal type of letter. Express your feelings in a way your friend (and maybe the grandchildren) will want to read it.
- Keep your friend as your focus and make it clear how much he or she means to you and make a difference in your life.
- Warmth and sincerity go well together.

Ponder how you might enhance your letter by decorating your writing paper with hand drawn pictures or doodles, or perhaps including a photograph or a memento to strengthen the bond between you both. Search online or in reference books for a suitable verse or quote to add to your sentiment.

Love Sample 1

29th January 2012

Dear Mandy,

No sunrise can ever bring so much warmth to the morning as your smile does when you wake. Dull and cold days are banished while your face radiates such a joie de vivre. I feel blessed to be part of your life. You have made our house such a happy home. Our children adore you (except when you wear your room-tidying-face) and they grow more like you each day.

Your selfless, hardworking nature is a true inspiration to us all and I am so happy to be with you – after all they do say opposites attract! The last twenty years have brought us closer. I love you more now than at any time in the past and am happy that I know this will continue day by day.

Yours forever,

Roger

The first sample was from partner to partner. The next sample is written to a best friend. A different approach is used as you would expect but nevertheless this is still a love letter.

Love Letter Sample 2

December 12, 2013

Dear Anne,

Nowadays the word friend appears to have so many meanings. Some people claim to have countless numbers of friends; some they have never even met! No matter what people think or say, you can only have one best friend, the one that can always be counted on. My best friend has always been you.

How we have laughed and cried together, shared secrets, dared the dares and been the reflection in the mirror for each other. I have always listened to –but not always liked – your advice, especially when you stop me from making a fool of myself. I know you have my best interest at heart and for that I am truly grateful.

You have always been there for me through school, through work, and throughout my marriage – Emma knows how special you are to me and has often told me she wished she had a friend like you too. I sometimes wonder what life would have been like without you being there. Who would have helped me with my homework? Who else would have gotten me into so much trouble in our teen years? Yet, here we march into our fifties still watching out for each other.

You are the best friend anyone could ask for. I want you to know that I love you dearly and thank you for always being there ready to stand shoulder to shoulder. I hope that your children and ours are as lucky as us in finding a lifelong friend.

So, despite how many friends others claim to have I would not trade you for a million friends because you are my best friend.

Forevermore,

Tony

Lifelong friends take, as you might expect, a life time or greater part of it to develop. The value of their friendship grows with us day by day and has the resilience to withstand any blows dealt by life's darker moments.

Daring Deliveries

You have written your letter, doodled and drawn your pictures, added your enclosures, decorated the envelope. If you are able to deliver it by hand then do so, if not then post it. Be imaginative on where you can secretly place your letter for discovery. Failing any imaginative flare you could just walk right up to the person and give it to them but that would detract from the surprise.

Here are a few ideas for you to start thinking about:

- ❖ Placing it on their car seat
- ❖ Ask a trusted friend to place it somewhere at their work e.g. on their desk.
- ❖ Perhaps put in a larger more official looking envelope and post it to their workplace or similar.
- ❖ In a coat pocket
- ❖ On the bath taps with a small piece of chocolate
- ❖ In the garden work shed
- ❖ Inside a book they are reading

You get the idea.

Chapter 17

A Letter of Curiosity

It is a miracle that curiosity survives formal education.
~ Albert Einstein ~

Curiosity, our lifetime companion, stands accused of a feline fatality, but suppose the murder never really happened. Imagine we discover the above said victim had escaped death. The cat is out of the bag! How do we treat curiosity now?

The Mechanics of the Argument
Is this thinking outside the box? No, as a thought experiment ponder all the things that might have happened if our thoughts are directed into the box especially if our cat is in there too.

So What?
So what exactly is a letter of curiosity? Well, there is no such thing; and yet, there is. You might be thinking this is more like a letter of confusion; we best clear this up as best we can. What we are really talking about is how to introduce more curiosity into our letters.

Words for Letters

On occasion we outpour events and accomplishments onto our reader, diminishing their attention and leading them to the concluding thought of 'so what?' Their interest wanes because we are not *sharing* our thoughts with them but instead are speaking from the land of me, myself, and I.

Liberate the reader from your ego drudgery and arouse their curiosity. Encourage an inquiring response. Do you think drab words will fuel your friend's urge to reply in an engaging manner? Plan the kind of letter which encourages the type of reply you would like to receive.

Let us move straight to a couple of sample letters to show you how this can be done. You will need your pencil, scrap paper, and notebook handy. Go fetch the shoebox.

Letter of (non)Curiosity Sample 1

Pretend you are Mark and you receive this letter.

> *January 14, 2012*
>
> *Dear Mark,*
>
> *I am thinking about joining a gym next week. It looks great; there are fitness classes each Monday, Wednesday, and Friday. I have chosen Monday 6-7, Wednesday 7-8, and Friday 5:30-6:30. Perfect! This will be good for me. I will be able to leave work earlier on Friday to make sure I get there in time. I have been reading about the benefits of exercise on the internet. Another benefit is that it will leave my weekends free so I can still shop and get the usual stuff done.*
>
> *Take care,*
>
> *Cathy*

How would you reply to this? Think a little about what you might say instead and jot down two or three sentences. How much sincerity is the in the closing 'Take Care'? This is not really a letter; more of an announcement. Do you find it engaging?

Okay, let us try a different approach with the same people and the same situation. Let us entice Cathy's pen down a different path.

Letter of Curiosity Sample 2

January 14, 2012

Dear Mark,

Christmas always leaves the unwanted gift of a few extra pounds. ☺ Where do they come from? Probably the work of Santa's mischievous elves during deep slumber time. No matter, the numbers on the scales are up; the wardrobe choices are down.

I have stumbled across a secret way to undo this mischief...

Your friend,

Cathy xx

I hope your shoebox is still handy. Two more questions for you to answer. How does this differ from the first letter in engaging your attention? Reflect on what Cathy has given you and contemplate how you might reply. Once more jot down two or three sentences. In addition, compare this reply with the one you scribbled for the previous sample. This exercise is useful to help us plan out how you write your letters.

Throw them a bone!

In the second sample Cathy is piquing curiosity in Mark towards her intended actions. Mark will want to know more and will respond with questions thus evidencing his curiosity. Questions are also a way to arouse curiosity. The wording is important.

Experiment with different ways of engaging your reader. Plan on expressing your thoughts in a way your friends will be able to easily reply. Prior to stowing your letter into your envelope read it one more time to ensure it encourages a reply

Expressing Curiosity

Before we move onto exploring questions further, heed this advice. If you have a lot of questions you must ask in relation to a specific topic, your reader will find it much clearer and easier to reply if you write them all on a separate sheet and make reference to that sheet rather than include them in the body of your letter. You may be planning a holiday and need more information. The separate sheet prevents the body of your letter from looking like an interrogation. Your friend ought to reply with the answers on a separate sheet too.

The next sample shows how we can express – rather than arouse – curiosity.

Letter of Curiosity Sample 3

April 23, 2012

Dear Sandra,
   Rumor has it you are buying a new car. I am intrigued and wish to know which one you have chosen. Which side of the fence did you come down on – the compact or the SUV?
   We will all miss 'Old Betsy'. She is a car of so many fun memories.
   The suspense is driving me mad - no pun intended! What have you replaced her with? And the name? WHO is your new car? Tell me everything!

Write soon,

Pauline

In sample 3 Pauline does not appear invasive nor is she prying. The way she expresses her curiosity is supportive, warm and carries a personal touch. Pauline has made it very easy for Sandra to reply.

Arousing Curiosity

Curiosity has no shape, does not play by the rules, and takes no sides.

Circumstances themselves can arouse curiosity. We do not necessarily have to create a mystery to make our friends inquisitive. The dynamics of a situation can do much of the work for you. The trick is to spot them and use them.

The next sample is very short and not even to the point or is it? The scenario is that Thomas would like to get to know his college friend Lynda much better but is unsure how to approach her. He knows she like animals especially horses but not much more than that.

Letter of Curiosity Sample 4

November 3, 2012

Dear Lynda,

Horses fall into the class of quadrupeds. They eat hay too.

Thomas

Even though this letter breaks so many of the 'technical' rules and guidelines of letter writing, it still works. If Lynda receives this as a handwritten letter in a matching envelope posted to her house her curiosity should be sky high. Thomas has made a special and individual effort for her despite only writing a few words.

Chapter 18

A Letter of General Correspondence

Letter writing is the only device for combining solitude with good company.
~ George Gordon Byron ~

The freestyle of letter writing has no ties with any particular occasion. Has no specifics-related purpose and yet is purposed. This letter is written from one friend to another to stay in touch and to keep the friendship alive. You can include or exclude whatever you like. Your letter might give specific news, ask advice, ask questions, discuss a holiday, express your feelings on a topic; the choice is yours.

This letter is possibly the most frequent type of letter we write or receive from our friends. Distance is a catalyst for this exchange of letters. We like to stay in touch with people who have moved away or perhaps children who are at university. However, distance is not the only catalyst; we may just want to write to a friend because we know they would appreciate the letter.

Format

How do you format a letter that is regarded as freestyle? The principles from all the previous chapters still apply. I recommend you always put effort into preparation for writing to your friends. They will enjoy reading it and appreciate your effort.

Once you have brought your shoebox to the table and settled down to write, try these simple steps:

- List the topics you would like to cover.
- Are you combining types of letters? If so, refer to the appropriate chapter.
- Will you need enclosures? Have them ready.
- What type of reply would you expect from your friend?
- Are there any questions you would like your friend to answer? Ensure you repeat or remind your reader at the end of the body of the letter.
- Briefly outline the order of your topics.
- Start writing!

You can combine one of the earlier letter types into your letter. For instance you could be updating a friend with news you know they will be interested in and also include an invitation or encouragement.

General Correspondence Letter Sample 1

June 3, 2013

Dear Samuel,

Thank you for the beautiful flowers you sent for my birthday. They made the day even more special. I can smell their scent every morning when I wake.

Isabel, my cousin, is coming to stay with me for two weeks in July. I have not seen her for two years. Would you like to meet her? You will like her, she is such fun.

I was thinking about joining a book group. Do you still attend the one you joined last year? The last time you mentioned it, you said you were enjoying it and the people were fun. There is one held here monthly at the library but I don't know much about it or anyone who attends it. Would you be able to pop over and come with me for moral support to one of their meetings? I will cook dinner for you as recompense for your help. If I don't feel happy I guess I can join your group. It's not that far to drive and would make more of a night of it.

Two weeks ago Dave and Jo went off to Europe for the summer; no doubt that will be an eventful trip. Jo was excited about France – she has been on some sort of crash course and is keen to speak as much French as possible. They said they would have a party when they got back in August so be prepared to hear from them.

How's your sister Mandy doing at her new job? Has she settled in okay? She did so well to be accepted –I heard there were over 200 applicants. Mind you, she has always been very intelligent and what a bubbly personality!

Once again thank you for the flowers. Let me know if you are happy to risk my cooking and come to the book club with me.

Smiles,

Eleanor

We have a Thank You, an Invitation, and a bit of news update all rolled into one. These are fun letters to write because you choose what you want to write about. Once you have a few friends to correspond with regularly you will enjoy writing and receiving letter like this every week.

Part 3

Chapter 19

Replying to a Letter

---

*To give counsel as well as to take it
is a feature of true friendship.*
~ Marcus Tullius Cicero ~

Reciprocity: I ask you to regard this word as 'the big R' because without it a FRIEND becomes a FIEND. Friendship works in a reciprocal manner. True magic lies between friends, generated by friends, for friends; a sort of circle of life thing. Friendships, without the reciprocity are merely an acquaintanceship or perhaps even less.

We must always reply to a letter from our friends unless the letter you received has asked you not to. Yes, there may be very plausible circumstances arise where a reply is not needed, but otherwise always reply to the sender.

What do I do?

Once again picture a meeting with your friend at the café with on-the-street tables. She arrives before you and waits at a table. You enter and she waves to you. As you approach her, she greets you and asks how you are. You reply with how you are. She will tell or ask you a question. You reply and then ask a question to her; in general this is how you reply to a letter too! It's part of an ongoing conversation.

The Basics

Let us go back to when you receive the letter. Unless you have something more pressing to do, sit in the most comfortable chair, with your favorite beverage and cupcake or goodie of your choice. Look at the envelope. Deep breath. Open the envelope. Take out the letter, check inside the envelope for enclosures. Okay, relax and read the letter. Take a sip of your drink. Read it again. Nibble on the cupcake and take another sip. Look at any of the enclosures again. Read the letter a third time but more slowly this time. Does it have a scent?

Settle further back in the chair and think about what has been written to you. How does it feel? Pop the letter along with any enclosures back in the envelope. Place it somewhere safe and carry on with the rest of your day.

Why such a ritual? Well, your friend has taken time to compose the letter for you, so reciprocate by taking your time to appreciate their effort and care for you. You know how the same food ingredients can be given to a number of people with access to the same equipment and yet one or two cooks will excel above the rest? They have the special ingredient of love!

Types of Reply

In Part 2 we looked at writing different types of letters; each with its own specific purpose. Are you now expecting to see thirteen chapters of specific replies? No? You can guess this answer by the number of pages left in this book!

Remember your reply is part of an ongoing written conversation. It still follows the general structure of the letter we covered in Chapter 3 and will morph into one of the letters we have already covered. Let us suppose that your friend has sent you a letter of congratulations; you may have raised some money for a charity. Your reply would acknowledge his letter, thank him for his support and then possibly invite him out.

So, the first letter offers **congratulations** (Chapter 5) your reply then issues a **thank you** (Chapter 7) and you move the conversation forwards with an **invitation** (Chapter 6). You will need to make the transition from thank you to the invitation a smooth one.

I expect you want to see a sample, so let us do that right now. Here is the letter of congratulations sample 2 from Chapter 5.

8th January 2014

Dear Meg, John, Cyn, and Bart,

Congratulations on achieving your Winter Goal of $10,000 after the sponsored hill walk on New Year's Day. This is such a splendid effort all round. Your third event of the program has already taken you past your target. Remember earlier in November when it looked impossible? What a turnaround! The training itself through the winter would have been daunting enough but to add the extra effort of asking people to part with their money required super human determination. But, you all did it!

Two senior citizens at the Drop-in shelter are so excited about the new equipment you can now install. They told us all about how this will improve the lives of less fortunate people. Good things are being said all over town about the shelter's accomplishments.

Well, you still have two events of your Winter program to go. "The Sounds of the 60s" will attract many more and as for the cake show, we drool with high expectation if last year's event is anything to go by.

No doubt many other felicitations are flying your way. You have done something very special for the community. Well Done! Well Done!

Big Smiles,
Clive and Will

Reply Letter Sample 1

12th January 2012

Dear Clive and Will,

Thank you for both your letter and your generous support. Your help has made all the difference and you can already see the improvements taking place at the shelter.

As you well know there are a few events still remaining this winter so be prepared to be hounded for further help.

John and I are so pleased we have decided to throw a small party at our house on the 22nd at 6pm. Nothing formal, we are making a sandwich buffet with a couple of hearty soups. I know it is a little short notice but we really hope you can make it. We have invited twelve people so you may have to park on the road. I have warned our neighbors and they have made their drive available too.

If you can make it, would you like to bring a dessert to add to the table? Cyn is putting together one her delightful sherry trifles.

Thank you so much for your support and I do look forward to seeing you both on the 22nd – we will have some fun!

Warm winter hugs,
Meg and John

The reply above as you would expect follows both the Thank You and Invitation guidelines but merges them into one letter. You may be wary of doing this initially but with a little practice you will soon get the hang of it.

Here is a little guide for you to follow. It is a simple process with steps to help you along.

Guidelines on Composing your Reply

Once you have read the letter from your friend several times and feel you would like to reply then it is time for your shoebox to appear.

- ❖ Take the letter you received and read it once more.
- ❖ On scrap paper make a note of:
  - ➢ What type of letter is this?
  - ➢ Have you been asked to do anything? If yes: what, when, where and with whom?
  - ➢ Have you been asked any questions? Be careful here because sometimes these can be well hidden.
  - ➢ Is anyone else involved?
  - ➢ Are there any immediate concerns or issues to be dealt with?
- ❖ Consider which tone you will use in the reply.
- ❖ Choose the letter types you want to use in your reply e.g. congratulations, comfort, apology etc.
- ❖ Plan the outline on scrap paper.
  - ➢ Opening
    - Thank your friend for writing.
    - Attract their attention.
    - Say what you are going to say.
  - ➢ Main Body
    - Answer questions.
    - Comment on any actions.
    - Include the next step.
  - ➢ Closing
    - Summarize what you have provided.
    - Re-ask any questions you have.
    - Warm finish.
- ❖ Write your reply using your outline. Take your time and choose the words you like to use to express your feelings.

And that is that!

Chapter 20

Personal Letter Writing skills

Writing is an act of faith, not a trick of grammar.
~ E.B. Wright ~

Personal letter writing is personal; there are no exams, no surprise tests; it only involves you, your friends and anyone else you choose to include. However, there is one question for you to answer. Why do *you* write letters? Only you can answer that, if you answer from your heart you are always right! Why do I do it? I write letters because I enjoy connecting with people and staying in touch. I suspect this is similar to the answer most people will come up with.

Rewards

You may have noticed that throughout this book the emphasis has been on the personal side of letter writing i.e. writing to people you know and care for. Although I did include a letter of recommendation, I have otherwise stayed away from covering writing to institutions, business letters, and the like. Those kinds of letters may be classed as personal because they are written by you but they are not personal because they are *impersonal* in their content and context. The letters we have covered together are warm and carry genuine affection for friends and family. Your letters are not just a form of correspondence; they are one of the pillars on which your friendships and relationships are built and remain strong. The way you choose to write your letters is up to you. No one will judge you or grade your letter. The technical do's and don'ts are secondary to the message. Your creativity in finding the warmest way of expressing your thoughts and feelings are the primary focus. Samples have been provided to suggest paths you can take but ultimately this is your journey.

Templates

Sometimes we let rules and regulations back us into a corner and we end up doing nothing. Doing nothing is not an option! Sorry, but you are better than that. You are reading this chapter because you want to write. So write! Don't let rules and regulations stop you from you expressing yourself to your friends. Become a rebel! Aim the pen at the page and shoot from the heart!

Templates may offer a solution to you if you are completely stuck on what to say. The internet has plenty of sites with templates available for writing in all sorts of scenarios. This is all well and good if you are looking for a quick 'how to' fix. However, after you have started writing some of your own letters first have a look at a few templates from different sites and see what you think. How well do they compare with your personal style? Do they carry the warmth of message that your letters do?

Your Style

Many opinions and fads relating to what should and what should not be included in letters are available. It is confusing at times and certainly disconcerting for anyone writing letters for the first time.

Despite all these opinions you will develop your own skills and be able to write any letter to anyone. I hope that this book has helped you learn to fish rather than given you fish. Maybe I will

Words for Letters

cover the subject of impersonal letters in a subsequent book. Nevertheless, it always pays to undertake thorough preparation and research when writing a letter. Be yourself, develop your own style and deliver what needs to be delivered in the best way you feel is appropriate.

No guarantees exist that your letters will always hit the mark but at least you will be writing the way you want to write rather than using other people's words. Somehow, you can tell the genuine letters from the others because of the originality.

Practice

I would like to share a practice technique with you. I still use it and know other experienced letter writers who use it too. This method can easily be adapted for use with other kinds of writing but for now we will stay with our personal letter writing.

Write a letter to yourself. You might find that a little crazy (probably because it is in a way) but it does help to develop your skills. I recommend you give it a try. If this feels weird, be assured; only you will know you are writing to yourself. Do not be concerned about what others may think; they have probably heard you talking to yourself from time to time!

Here's what to do. Imagine you are going to write to someone. You will need your shoebox.

- ❖ Pick a topic that is on your mind. Perhaps something that worries you or possibly an event or activity you are excited about.
- ❖ Browse through the previous chapters and pick one or more that suit your topic.
- ❖ What outcome from the letter would you like? Jot down a few notes.
- ❖ Using the selected chapters make a few notes and scribbles on scrap paper about what you would like to say. How do you want this letter to come across to the recipient?

Words for Letters

- ❖ Write the letter. In the salutation address to either yourself or the person you are planning on writing to. Leave a space where the date should go.
- ❖ Address the envelope to you. Put the letter into the envelope along with any enclosures (you will have fun writing the return address on this envelope!)
- ❖ Post it; yes, post it to yourself. If you cannot do this, for some reason, then put it somewhere you will not look at it.
- ❖ When it arrives in the post do not open it. Leave it for three days. No cheating or sneak peeks.
- ❖ Open it and read it.

Does it say what you thought it would say? Is this the same letter you remember writing? It might seem a little different. Does it say what you want it to say? Does it say things in a way you wanted to say them?

Why might it appear different than what you thought you were writing? Has the envelope protected the letter since you sealed it or not? You may suspect that words have mischievously exchanged places on the paper while waiting patiently in the envelope; but that is not the case. Can written words escape from the paper through a small gap in the envelop seal? They were in your head and you were sure you wrote them but they are not there now; very mysterious!

What happened to that warm and comforting tone you wrote the letter in? The cold may have pierced the envelope and cooled it a little.

Consider how the letter differs from what you thought was said. What changes could you make to recapture the thoughts you meant to put there. Rewrite the letter by making changes that bring it into line with your original intentions.

Finally, look at the stationery to determine if this is the most appropriately fitting option you have. You may enhance the tone by changing the paper or ink color. There may be changes you could make as to how you addressed the envelope or perhaps include a decorative sticker to the back of it.

Of course you may be happy with the letter as soon as you read it. This is why a blank line for the date was suggested. If this is the case and you are happy with the letter as it is, simply add the date, address a new envelope and post it!

I, and many others, find the above practice method does help to improve our writing skills. You may not use it for every letter but it certainly helps with those which are a little awkward to write.

10 Golden Rules of Letter Writing

1. Your letter focuses on your reader, not you. The topic is a way to create the focus.
2. The more effort you put into your letters, the bigger the rewards for your reader.
3. The bigger the rewards for your reader, the bigger the rewards for you.
4. You are unique; so are your letters.
5. Always include the date.
6. Keep the letters you receive; you will want to read them again someday.
7. Have fun and be grateful.
8. Before writing your letter, put yourself in your reader's position. Think about what he or she would like to read about in your letter.
9.
10.

You may wonder why 9 and 10 are blank. Those have been left for you to fill in. As your skills develop you will develop your own golden rules. When that time comes; add your rules to the list.

Chapter 21

Fun with Letters

Fun is good.
~ Dr. Seuss ~

We are almost to the end. Shall we have some fun as we head to the closing chapter? It is perfectly acceptable to decorate your letters and envelopes as you see fit as long as you do not interfere with the postal process or include any objects that may cause injury.

In the next few pages I will show you some basic ideas on how you may wish to add decorative interest or to perhaps ignore everything I stated in Chapter 3 and deliberately break the 'rules' (oh! you rebel) for effect and to give your friends a little something extra.

Please remember to be appropriate and avoid upsetting anyone. However, if you do, I would be grateful if you did not blame it on this book!

Writing letters will change your life, it has a certain magical aura about it which is hard to describe and people experience it in different ways.

In addition, you should be aware of the following:

5 (Almost) True Facts About Letter Writing

1. Letter writing enhances your looks. You will instantly become super attractive to everyone you meet.
2. Letter writing is a form of special physical exercise which will get you into the best shape of your life.
3. Letter writing makes you incredibly rich.
4. Letter writing enables you to speak to pens in a special language.
5. Letter writing will expand your footwear to unprecedented levels of comfort and style.

The final validations, approval, and recognition of these facts are still outstanding; nevertheless we are hopeful that this will happen soon.

In the meantime you will have to be content with the many happy hours you will spend writing letters to those who are special in your life. Let's not also forget the special moments you receive letters and enjoy them, and then enjoy them, again and again! Life can be tough sometimes.

For your perusal

I have included two sample letters and a sample envelope in this chapter. I hope you like them. You can have great fun (and frustration if you are like me and can't draw!) adding creativity to your letters.

These samples are in black and white but you can imagine the effect color may have.

Remember not to overdo the decorations, but do have fun amusing your friends with them.

Words for Letters
Fun Letter Sample 1
Surprise your friends by adapting a different lay out approach.

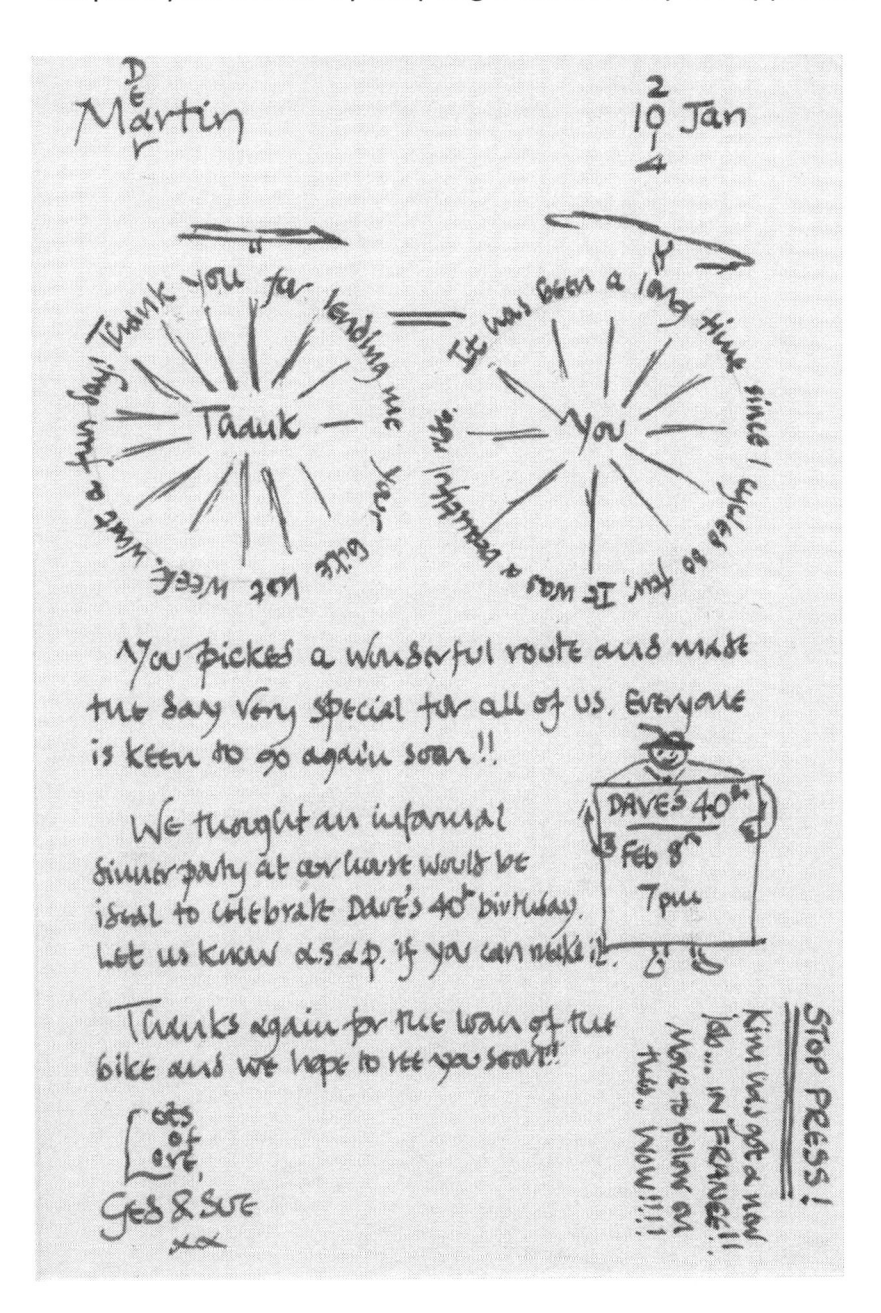

Fun Sample Letter 2

How about this?

Dear Marie,   Jan 20, 2014

Several years have sneaked past since we had such a fantastic time camping on the beach at Lakeside. Far too long! We must make plans IMMEDIATELY, so put down whatever you are doing and check your diary. There isn't a second to lose!

I am free most of May and all of June. Perhaps we could travel up on the Friday and return Sunday evening.

Yours-ready-to-start-packingly,

Liam

Words for Letters

Fun Sample Envelope

Do you like this envelope? Notice how the central area and top right corner are clear so the address can be easily read and the stamp easily affixed.

Chapter 22

Reading Letters

Friends share all things.
~ Pythagoras ~

Receiving a handwritten personal letter invokes our curiosity, whether it be nestling in our mailbox or thoughtfully placed somewhere to surprise us. We want to know who sent it, why someone has written to us, and what is inside the envelope. There is only one sure way of satisfying our curiosity; open it!

Stay Calm And Stay Safe

In this euphoric moment do not abandon all composure and attack the envelope until it yields its contents to you. Be careful when opening the envelope not to damage the contents. This can happen if the fold of the letter inside of the envelope is at the top rather than at the bottom, and you use a sharp letter opener to slit the envelope open. You would not be the first cut a letter in half neither will you be the last.

Letter openers are very useful but please be careful about using the sharper types. Do not leave it lying around if you have young children in the house regularly or just visiting. You really do not want anyone to incur injuries. Also, if you are the macho type, explaining to your friends that your hand is bandaged up and your arm is in a sling due to opening a defenseless envelope will not add any incremental value to your street credibility. People will talk about you and point you out. The sniggers you hear are not in your imagination. O shame!

Let us assume you have safely opened the envelope. Remove the letter and check if there is anything remaining in the envelope. Next, sneak a quick peek at the end of the letter to see if any enclosures were listed, and if so; were they actually included? Keep any enclosures with the letter.

Maximize The Experience

No doubt that at this stage your eyes are ready to gallop along the lines to see why someone has written to you. Alternatively, you could sit in your favorite chair, beverage in hand, and let your eyes stroll through the letter, soaking up each word and bask in your friend's attention.

Read it several times. Savor it. Put it back in the envelope along with any enclosures.. Place it somewhere handy, you will want to read it again later or even the next day. I suggest you do this because sometimes, in the heat of the moment, we may miss something that has not been directly said but inferred. Remember the exercise we did in the earlier chapter on improving our writing skills? The one where you wrote a letter and then read it much later to see if you had written what you thought you had written? Well, this is also true of the reading a letter. When we chat face-to-face, only a small percentage of the communication relates to the words. Other aspects such as facial expressions, gestures, and body language come into play. In a letter the tone and mood play a similar role, the words are chosen with more consideration. What do you sense beyond the actual written words? Mentally note which words have been chosen to represent your friend's thoughts and feelings. Further readings will help you detect any unsaid message.

Be mindful that not all envelopes carry happy messages; some bear unpleasant or sad news. The manner in which the envelope has been addressed can sometimes give clues to the nature of the content.

Archiving For Nerds

Once you have finished and replied to your letter, move it to your archives with all the other letters. This is how those extra shoeboxes you purchased come in handy to form a magnificent vault of stored correspondence; a social testimony to your life. In addition, if you have zealously purchased aforesaid archival containers; a variety of stylish footwear awaits to comfortably transport you to and from said archives.

You, or someone connected to you, may need or want to reference one of your previous letters at some future date. Rather than use the 'mound' storage technique (whereby you throw letters onto an already overburdened piece of furniture in the name of entropy), file them in order in your designated shoebox. Please avoid using the top of the refrigerator; we already know where that can lead, don't we?

Retrieving a specific letter can be arduous if they are all randomly stowed in the shoebox; similar to trying to find a specific pair of socks in an unsorted pile of fresh laundry when you are in a mad rush to go out. The problem is that you have to take the letters out of the envelope to see if it is the one you are searching for. What happens next is inevitable. You start reading a bit of one, a bit more, and then all of it. This trend repeats with the next letter and so on and so forth. Add in a little daydream or two, and before you know it you have missed meals, the kids have grown up and left home. Strange people you have never met before have moved in and claim that you are the squatter. They call the police, it all gets ugly, and you end up being allowed supervised exercise for one hour a day walking round a yard. Oh if only...

Yes, exactly, if only you had listened to your inner nerd and carried out these simple steps:

Words for Letters

- ❖ Take a sheet of paper or create a spreadsheet
- ❖ Create three columns
- ❖ Label the first column 'Ref'
- ❖ Label the second column 'Name'
- ❖ Label the third column 'Date' (yyyy mm dd format)

Archiving your letter is simple. Create an index for your archived correspondence.

- ❖ Write a reference number (starting with '1' is a simple and effective idea.) on the envelope perhaps in the bottom left corner.
- ❖ Record '1' in the first column.
- ❖ Add the name of the person who sent it in the second column.
- ❖ Add the date in the third column. Place the envelopes in reference number order.

As each letter is archived increment the reference number. Now you have an index of your letters and can locate them quickly thus avoiding the awkward alternative described a little earlier.

You might choose to add more functionality to this simple system and make wonderful and detailed advances in your own archival techniques by creating an intricately structured database relating to all aspects of indexing your correspondence. If you combine this with your ever-growing knowledge of component identification numbers and other specialist information we covered earlier; you can probably mark more weekend conventions on your calendar.

Chapter 23

The Closing

Action is the foundational key to all success.
~ Pablo Picaso ~

27th January 2014

Dear Reader,
  Thank you for sharing in this exciting world of personal letters. Your enthusiasm is the inspiration for this book so I hope you have enjoyed reading it.
  Use this book to help your friendships and relationships blossom by adding new ways of connecting with those you care for. Your skills will develop to match your passion with each letter you write or read.
  Letter writing is highly rewarding and while there are people like you penning their care and support to others, we all have a chance of happiness.
  To the future: many hearts will be grateful for the letters you will write and the love you will share.

Yours in gratitude,
Keith

Valediction

May your pen make many souls dance.

About the Author

On September 9th 1967 Keith Winnard attended his first day at a full time boarding school in a picturesque area of rural Northern England. Students were allowed home three times a year; letter writing was the only option for connecting with family and friends during term time. Luckily, the school curriculum included learning letter writing skills, and a weekly supervised class was allocated to write letters. The curriculum also included handwriting classes. You can imagine how much he enjoyed sharing his new experiences with his family and friends. They would reply and keep him up to date with what was going on in his home town. Letter writing has always been a part of his life - a very enjoyable part.

A successful career in Information Technology spanning over 35 years in technical, consulting, and managerial roles followed presenting many exciting and unique projects throughout the U.K. and Europe.

In more recent times he moved to West Michigan, and continues to write to friends and family both in the U.S. and in the U.K. who share the same enthusiasm for personal letter writing.

Made in the USA
Charleston, SC
01 June 2014